I0468164

COLORING BOOK OF
DINOSAURS
AND OTHER
PREHISTORIC BEASTS

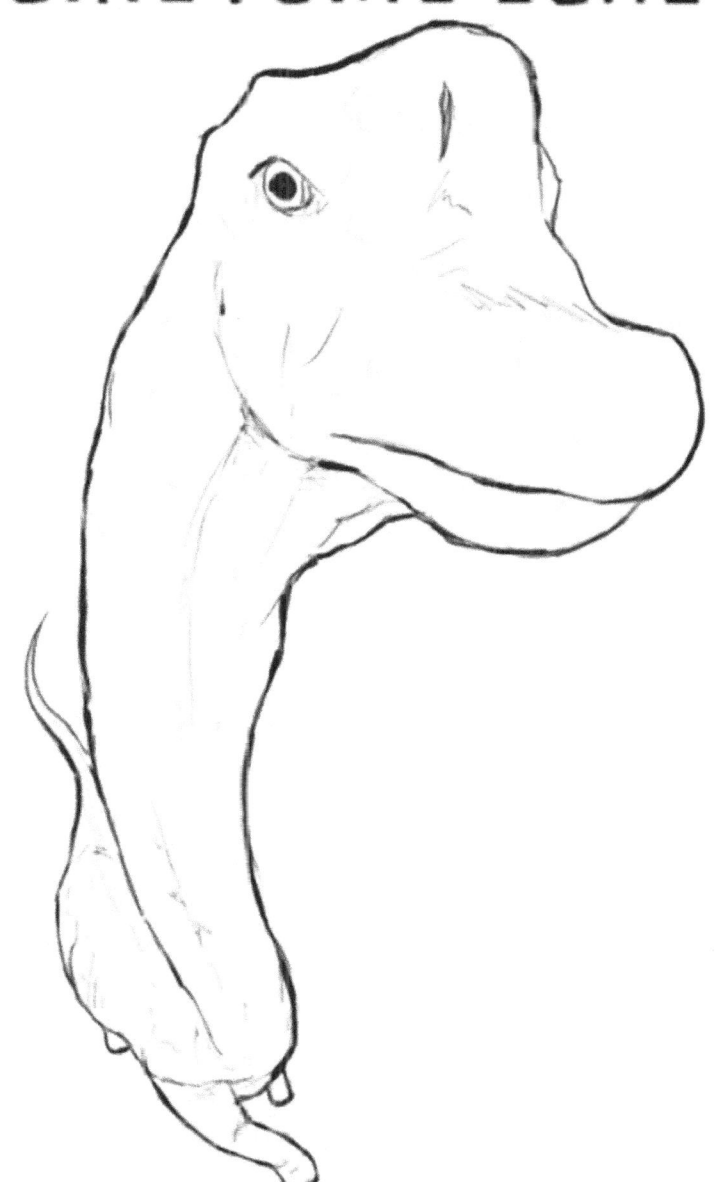

Illustrated by TC Mahala

It's usually Dinosaurs that will first capture the imagination of children. The thought that these monstrous beasts actually walked the Earth helps keep Dinosaurs in the minds of adults as well. This coloring book is for everyone, young or old, with original illustrations of Dinosaurs and other prehistoric beasts that don't fall under the same classification, but still bring a sense of awe. Duplicated to give multiple options for color schemes or different scenes or your own creation.

For updates on other products, like us on
Facebook @ Pickled Genius Projects

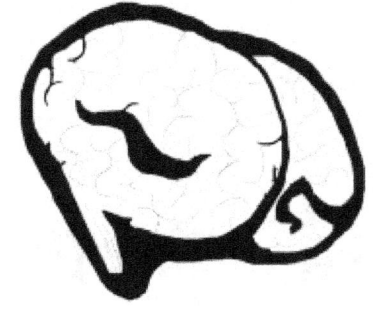

PICKLED GENIUS PROJECTS

HERBIVORES

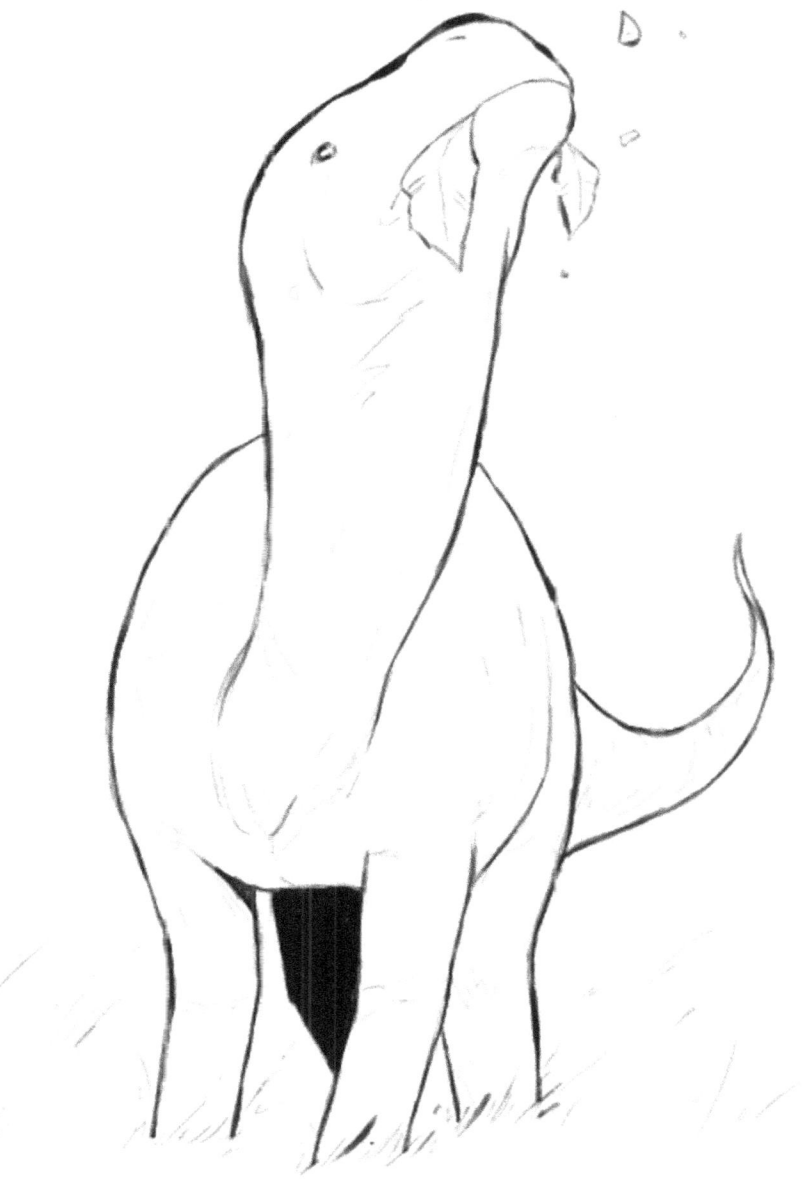

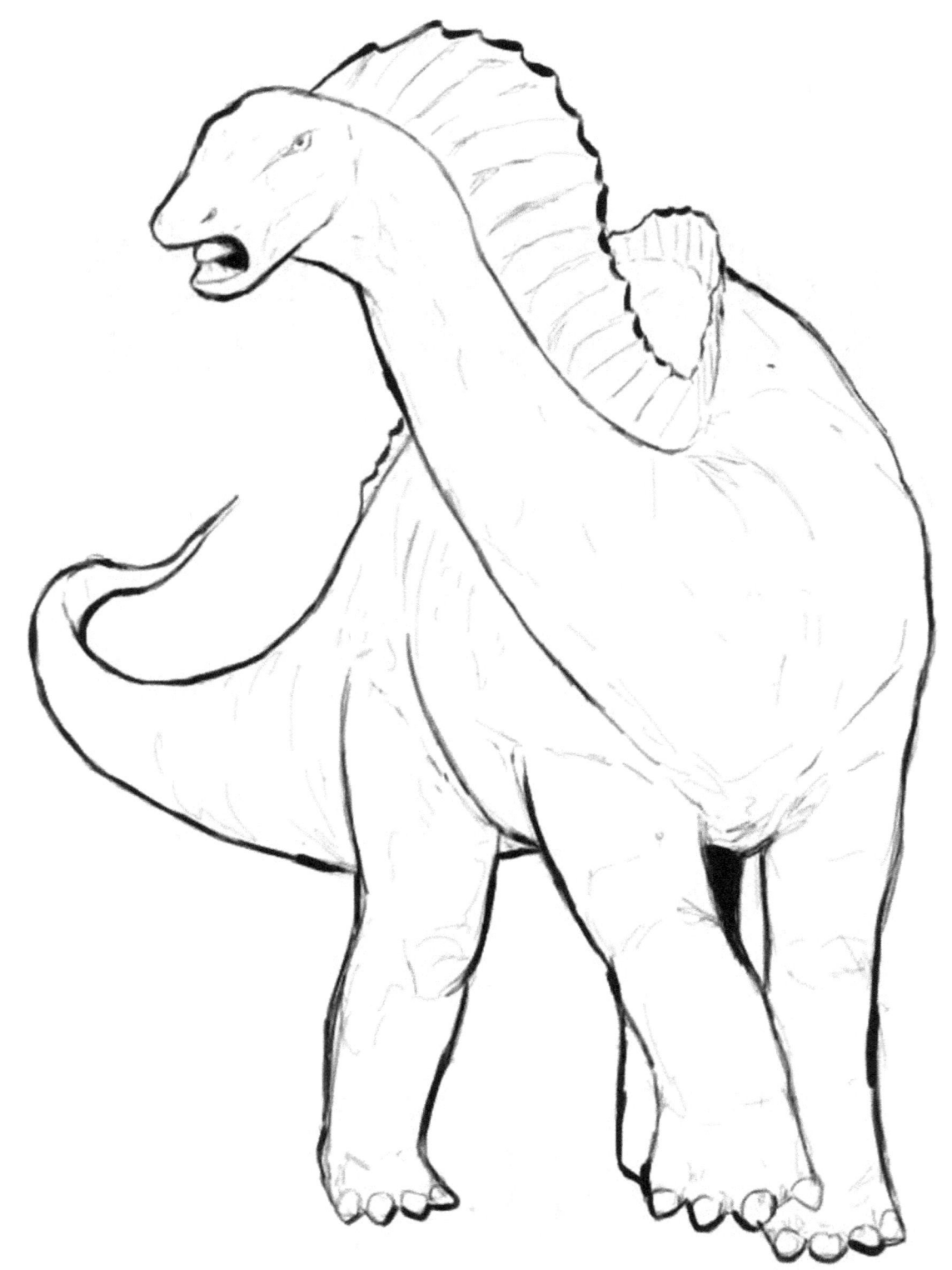

AMARGASAURUS

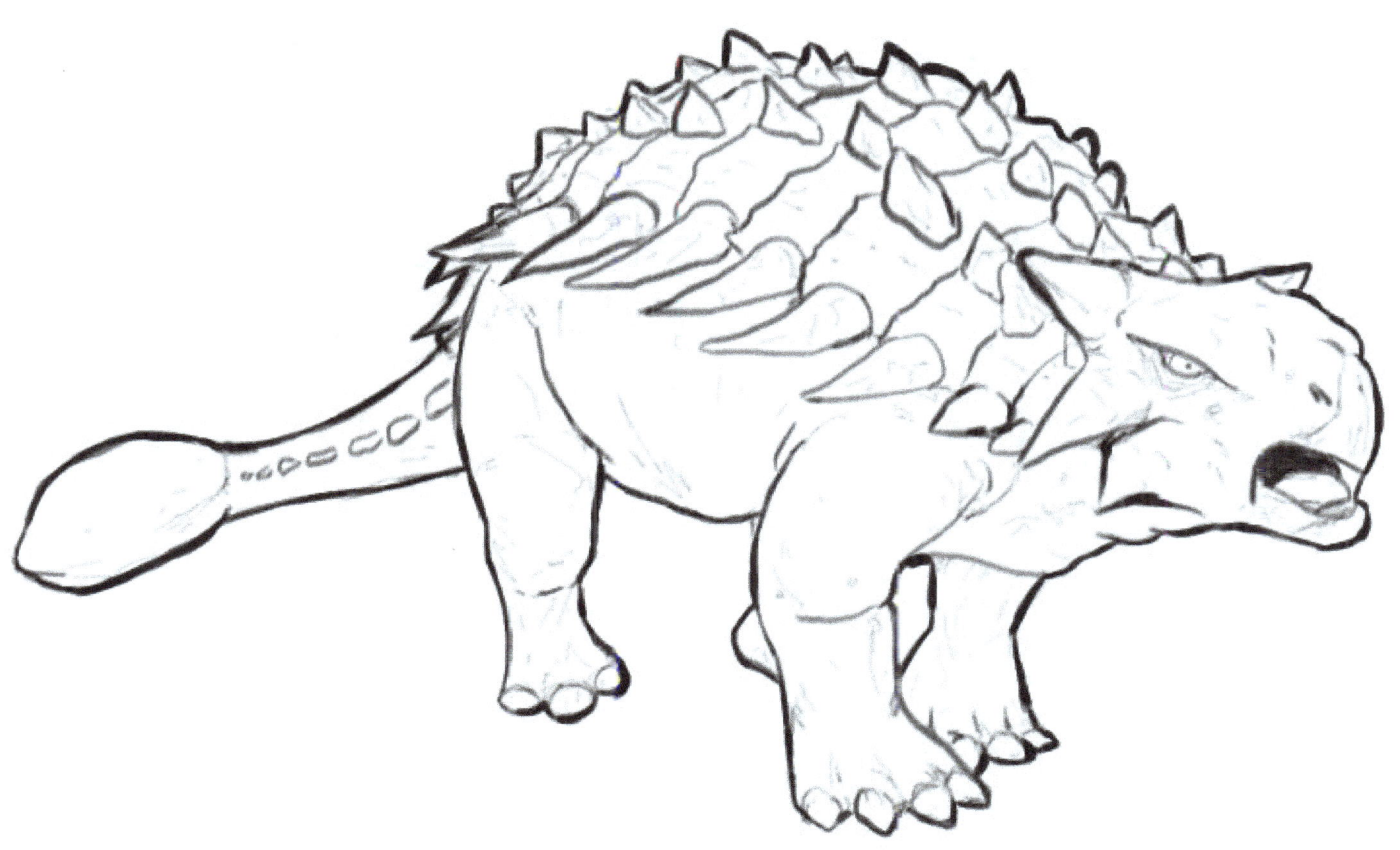

ANKYLOSAURUS

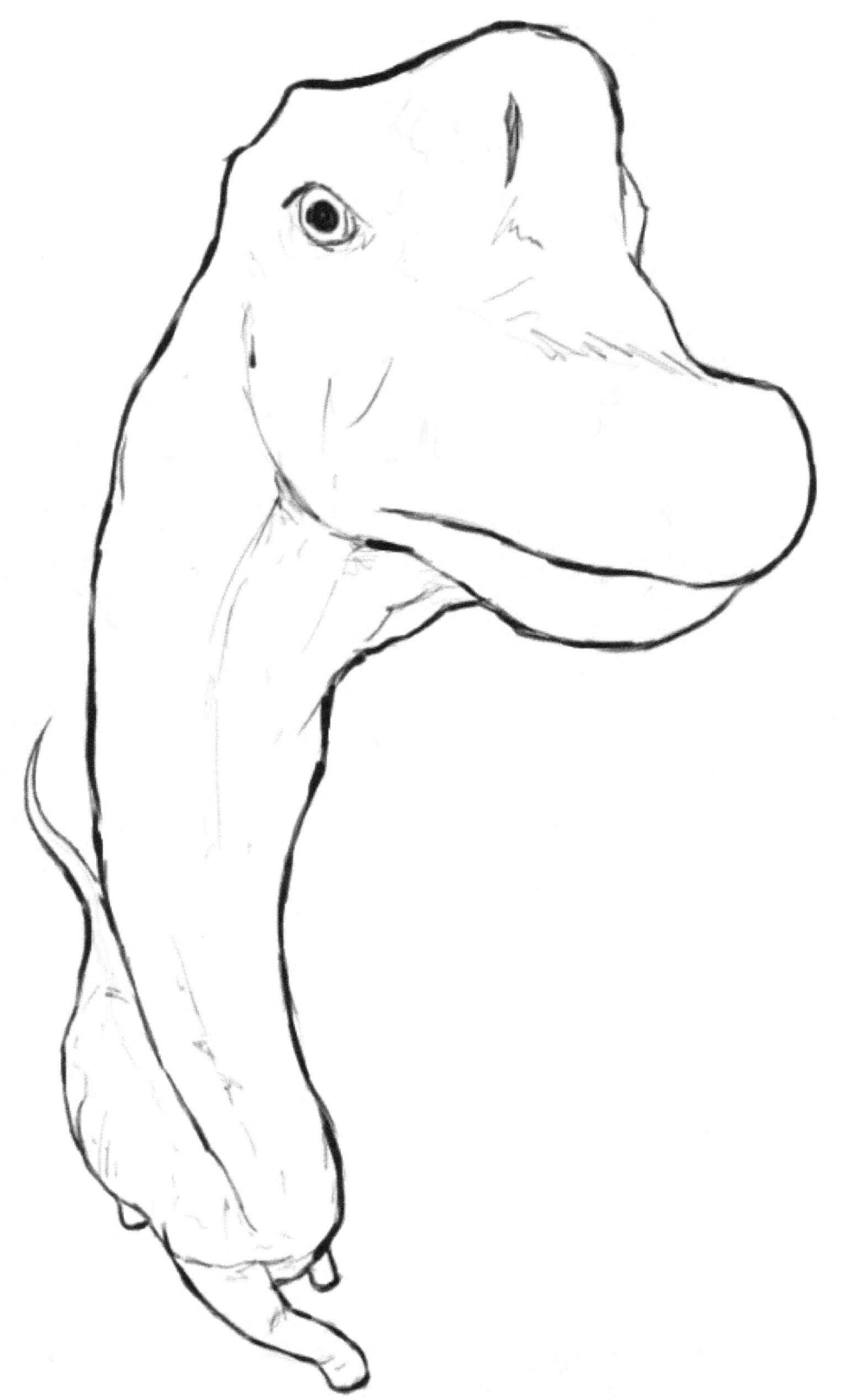

BRACHIOSAURUS

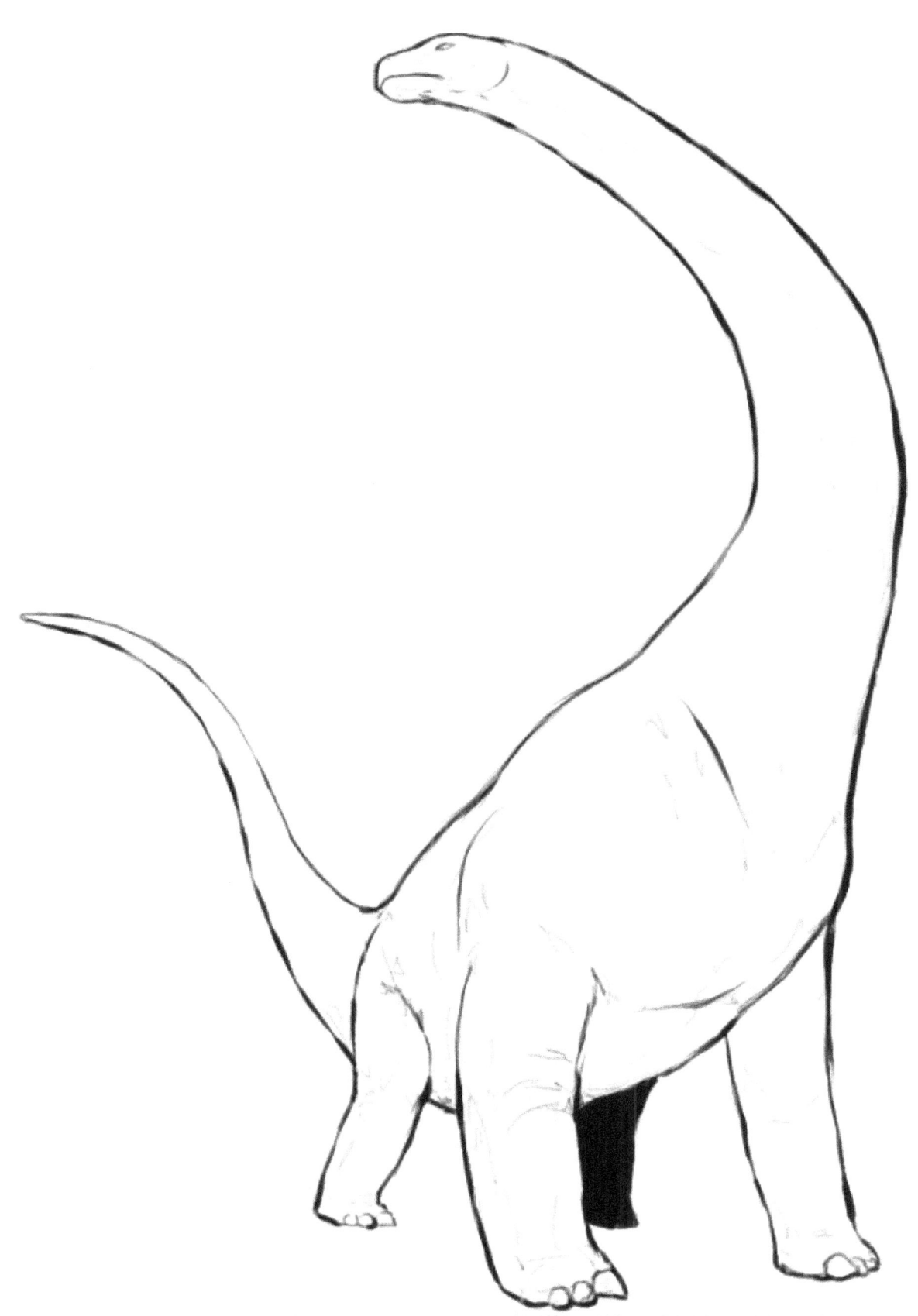

BRONTOSAURUS
(aka Apatosaurus)

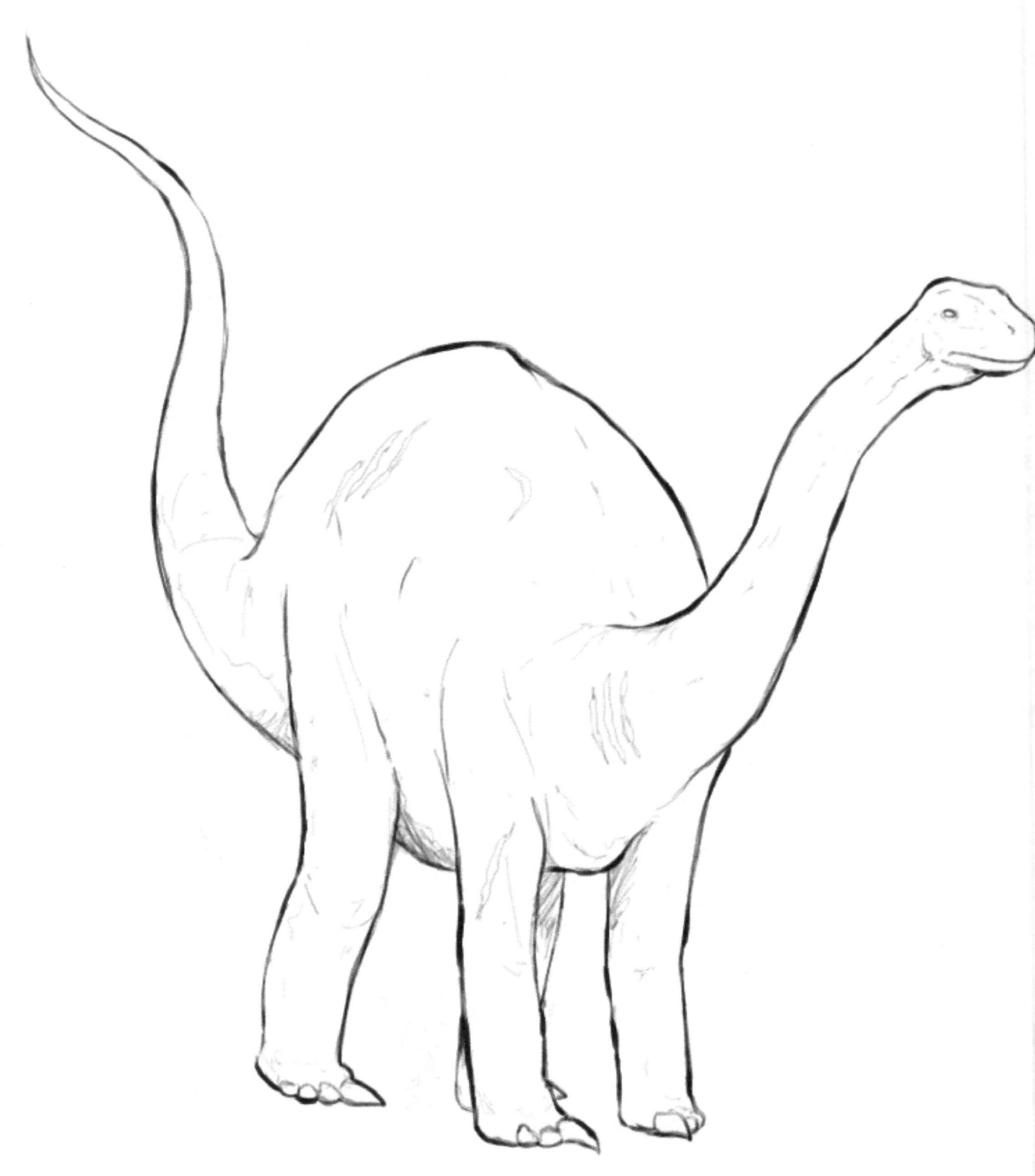

DIPLODOCUS

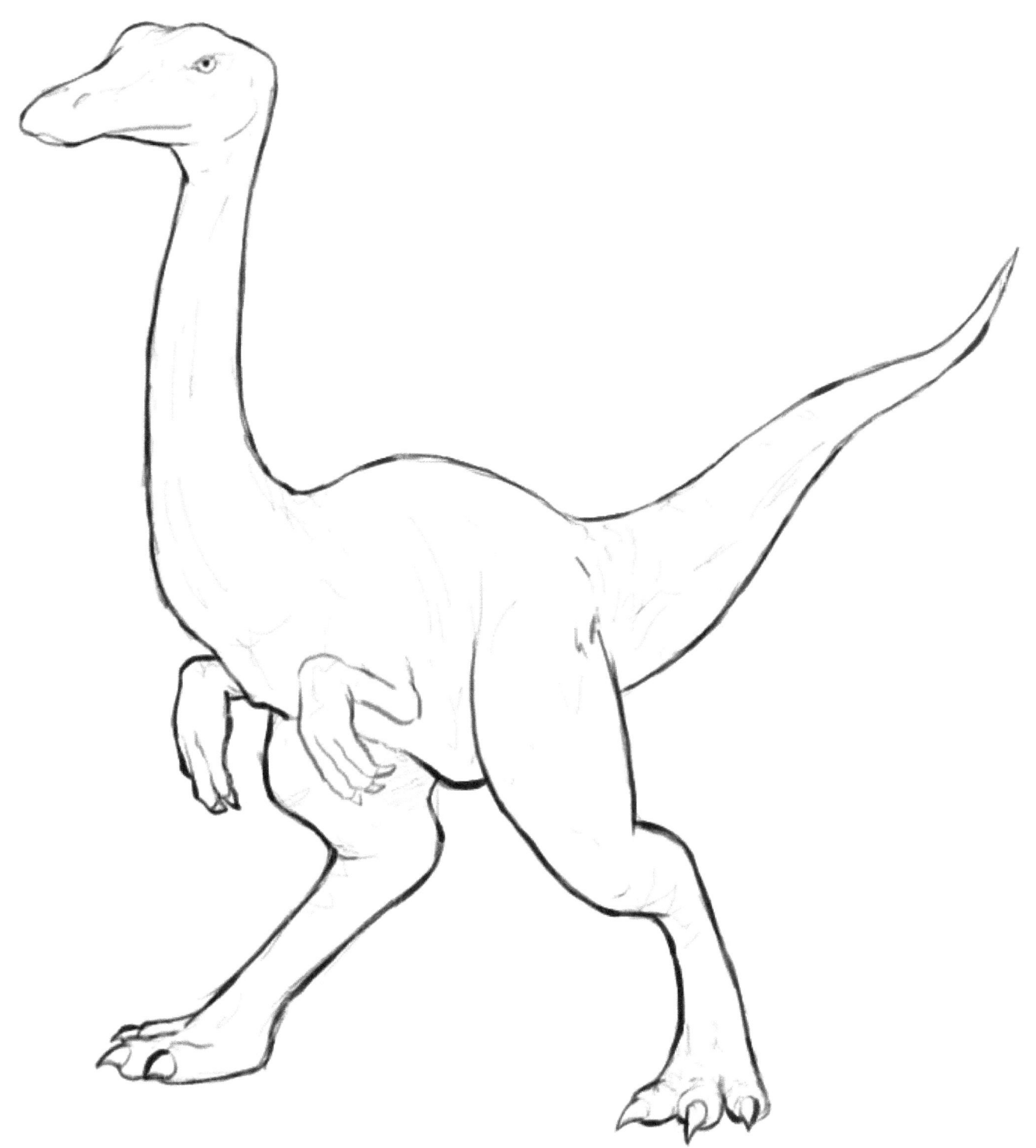

GALLIMIMUS

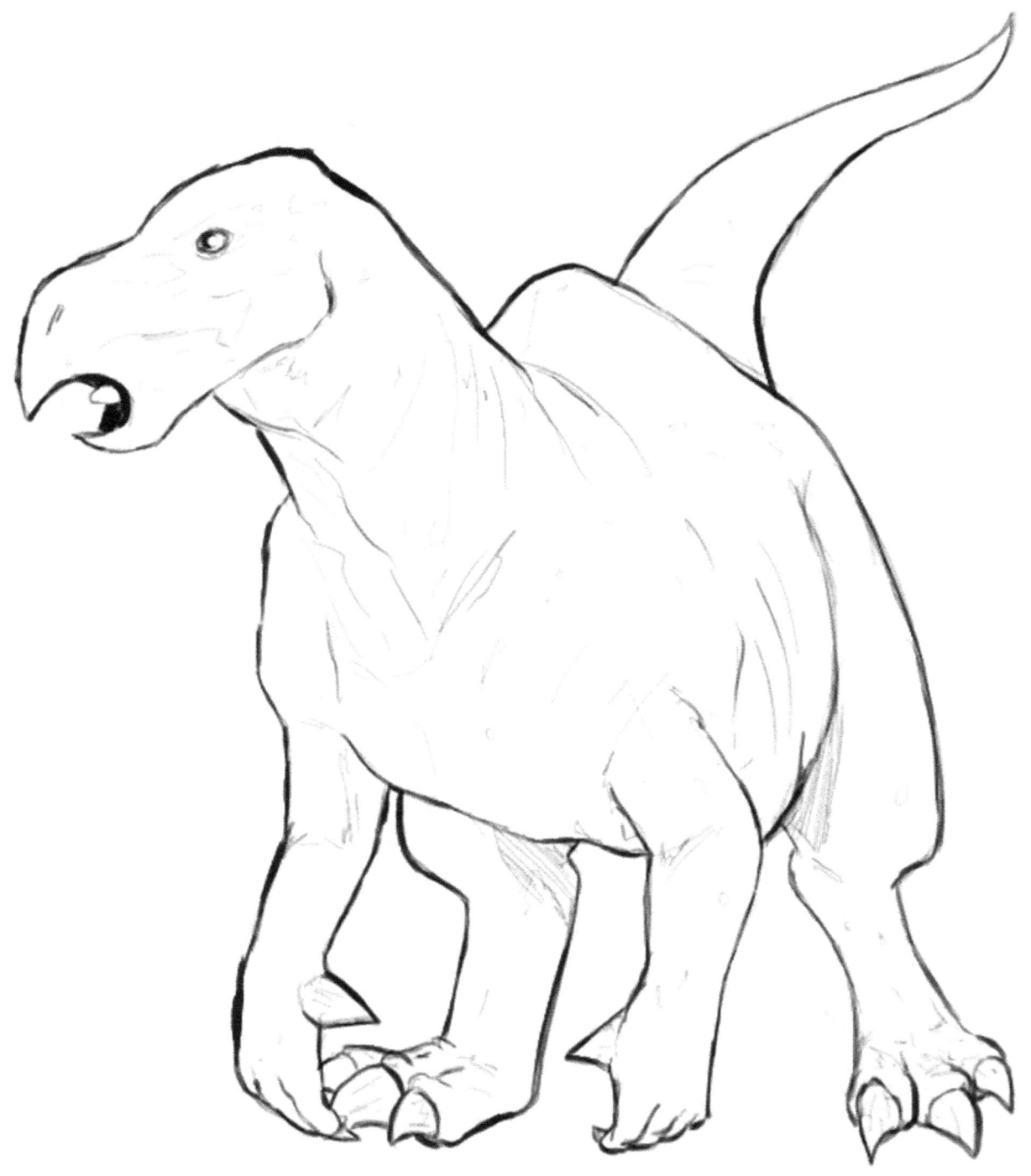

IGUANADON

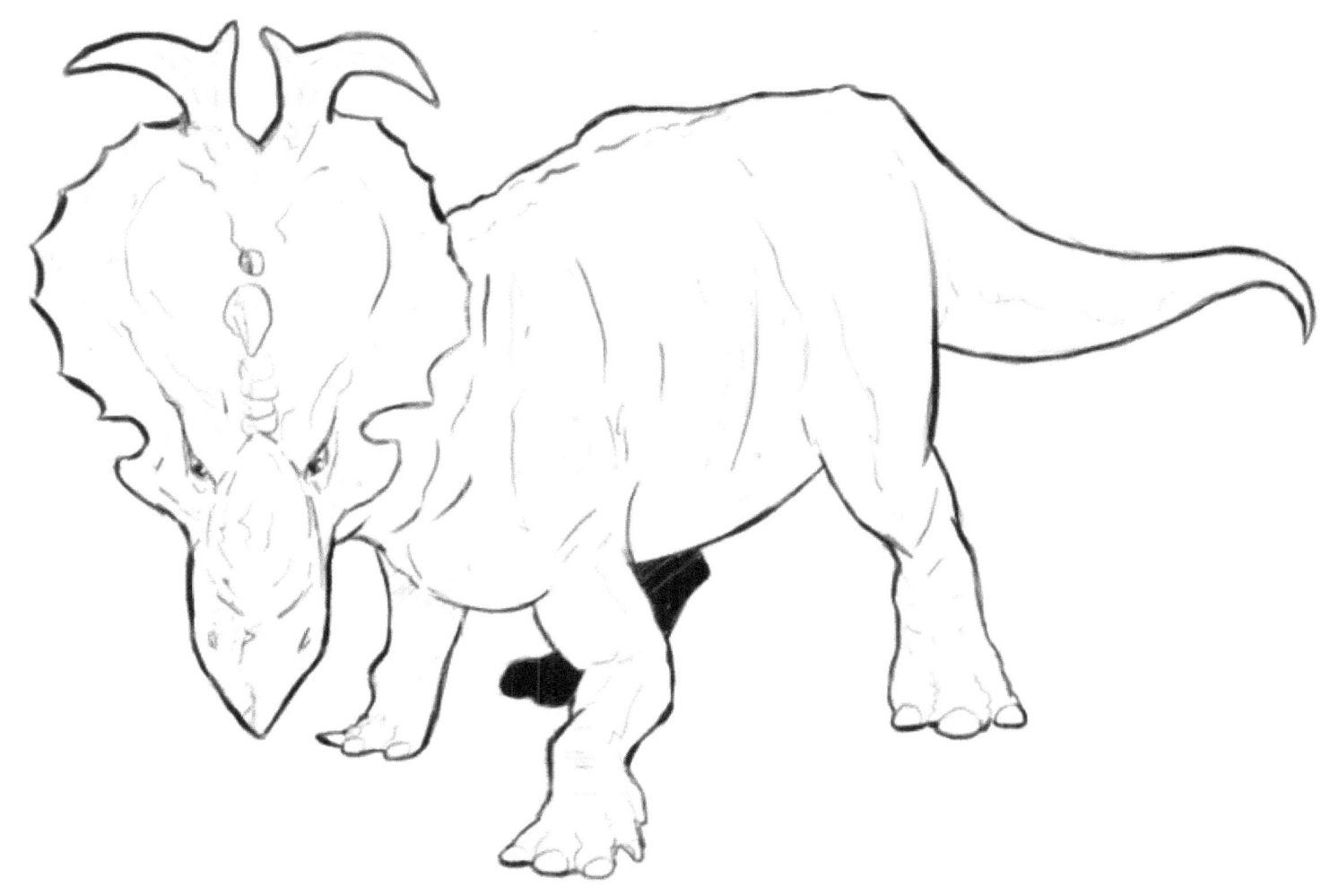

PACHYRHINOSAURUS

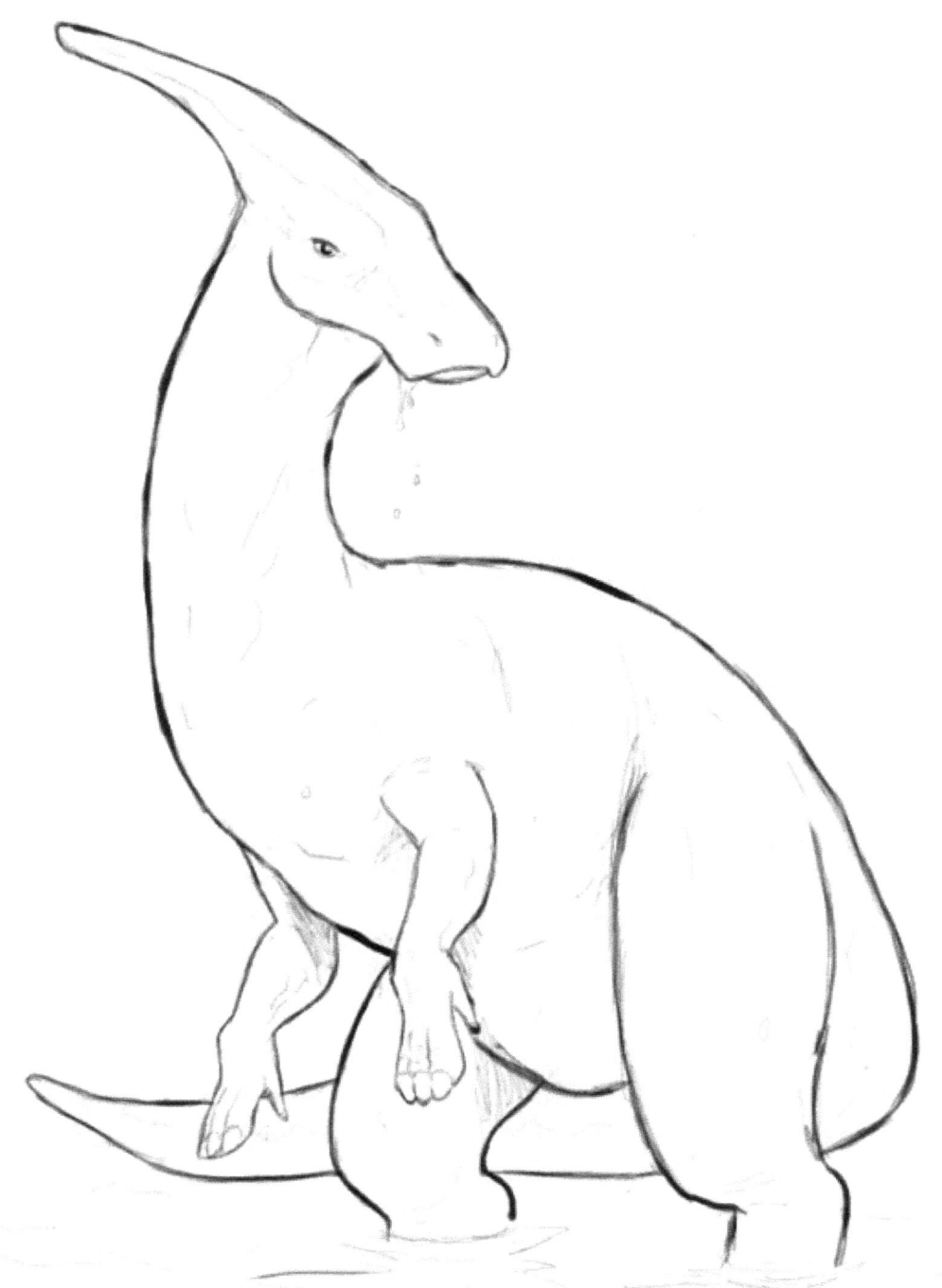

PARASAUROLOPHUS

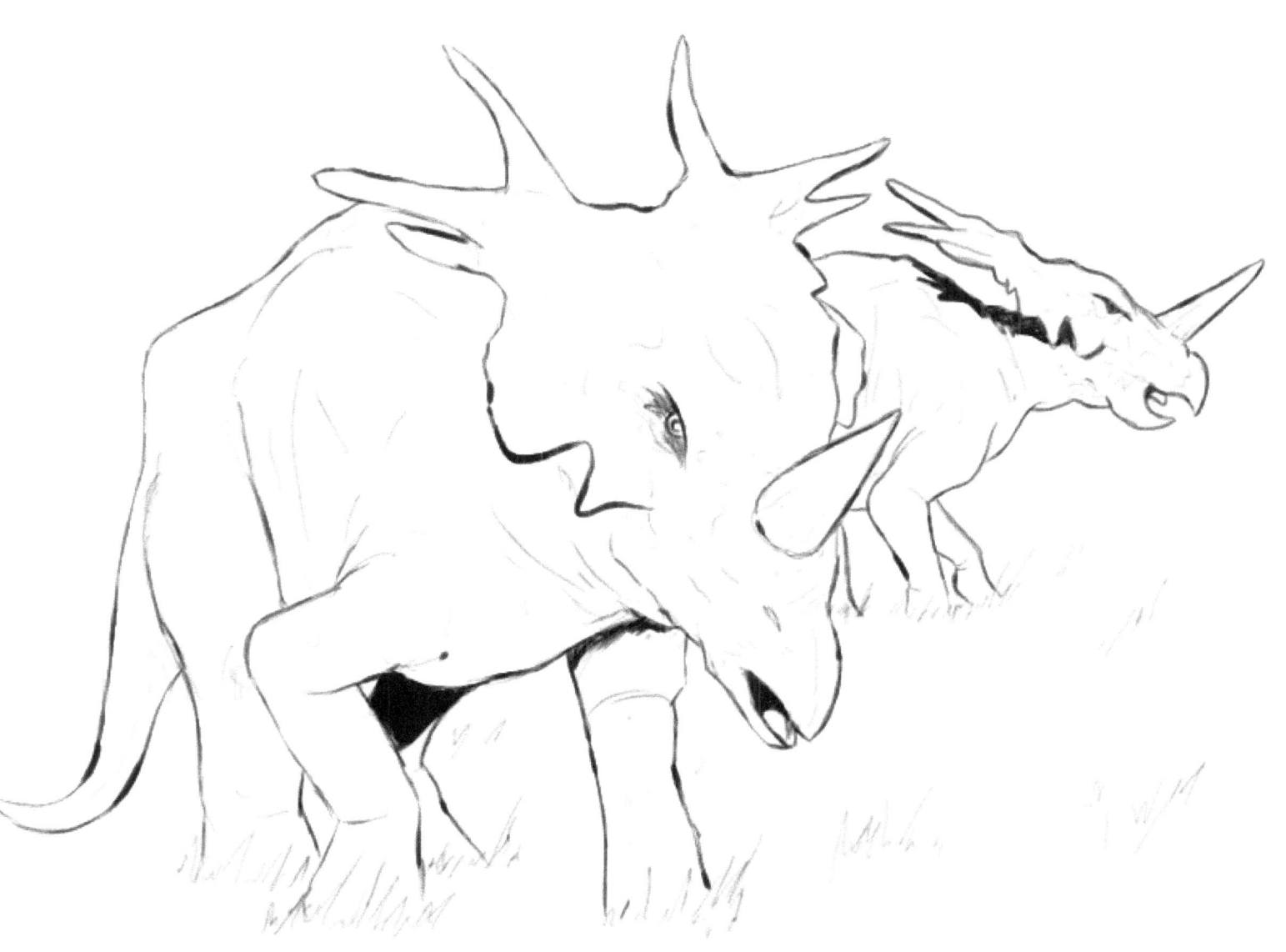

STYRACOSAURUS

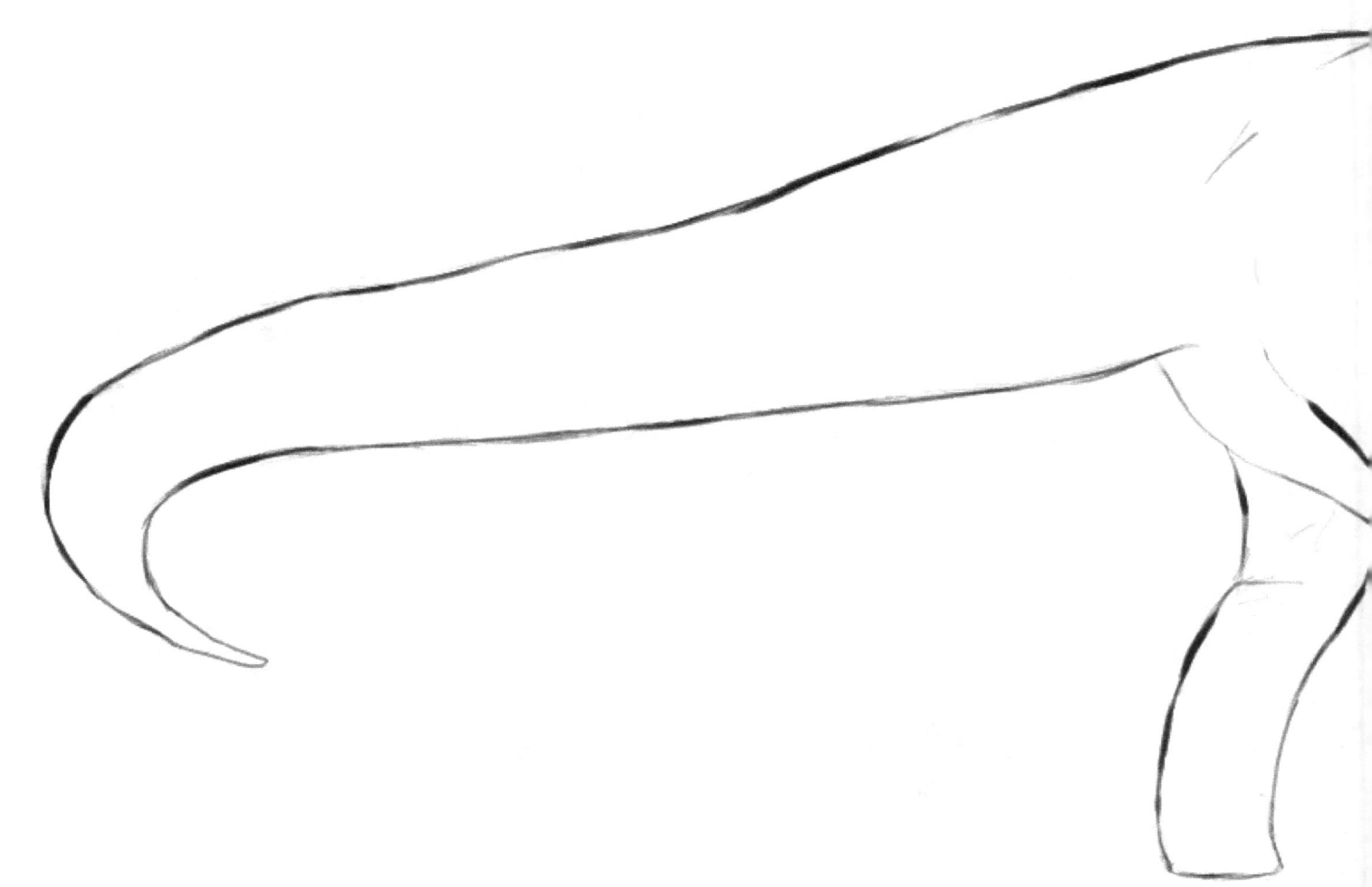

PATAGONIAN

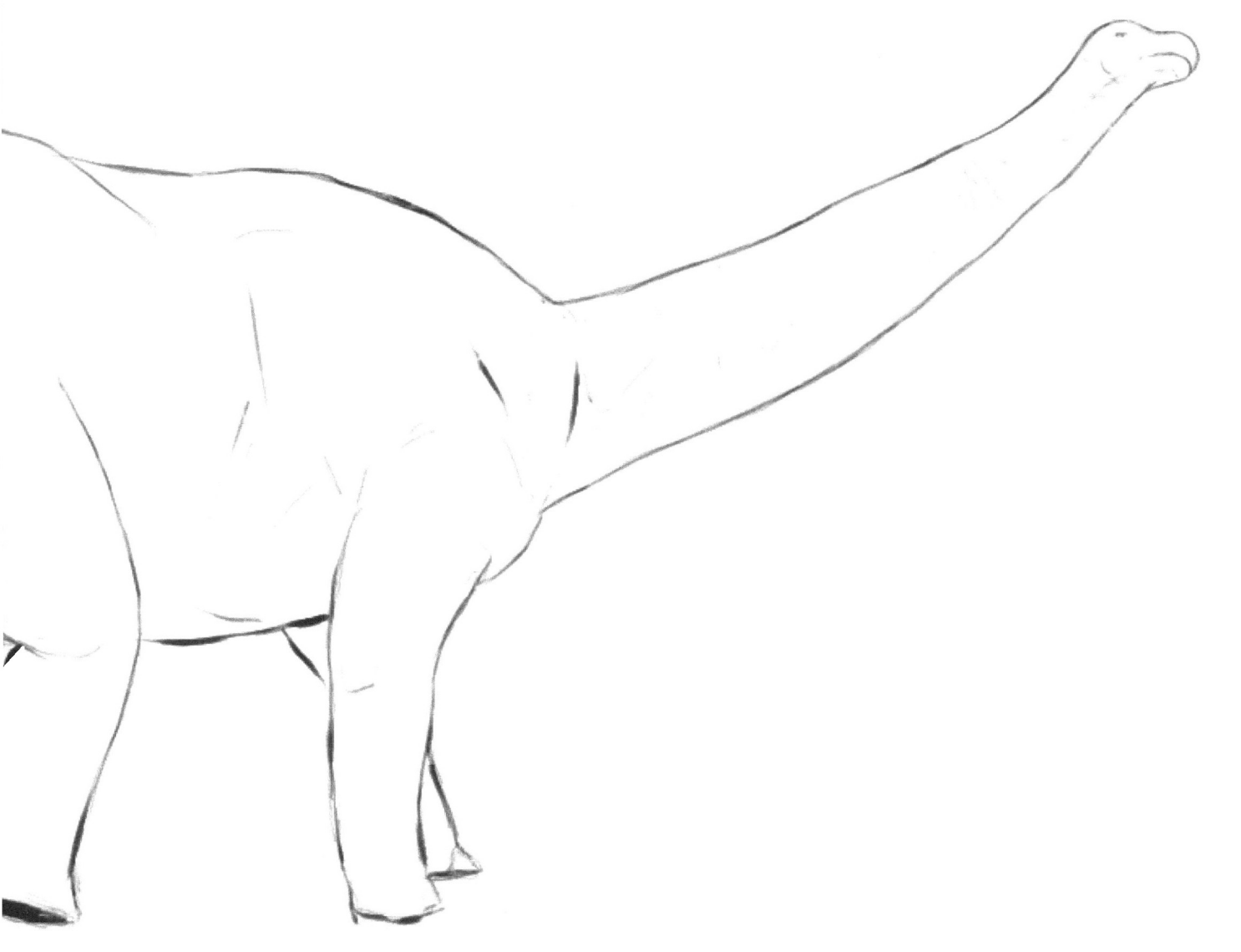

TITANOSAUR

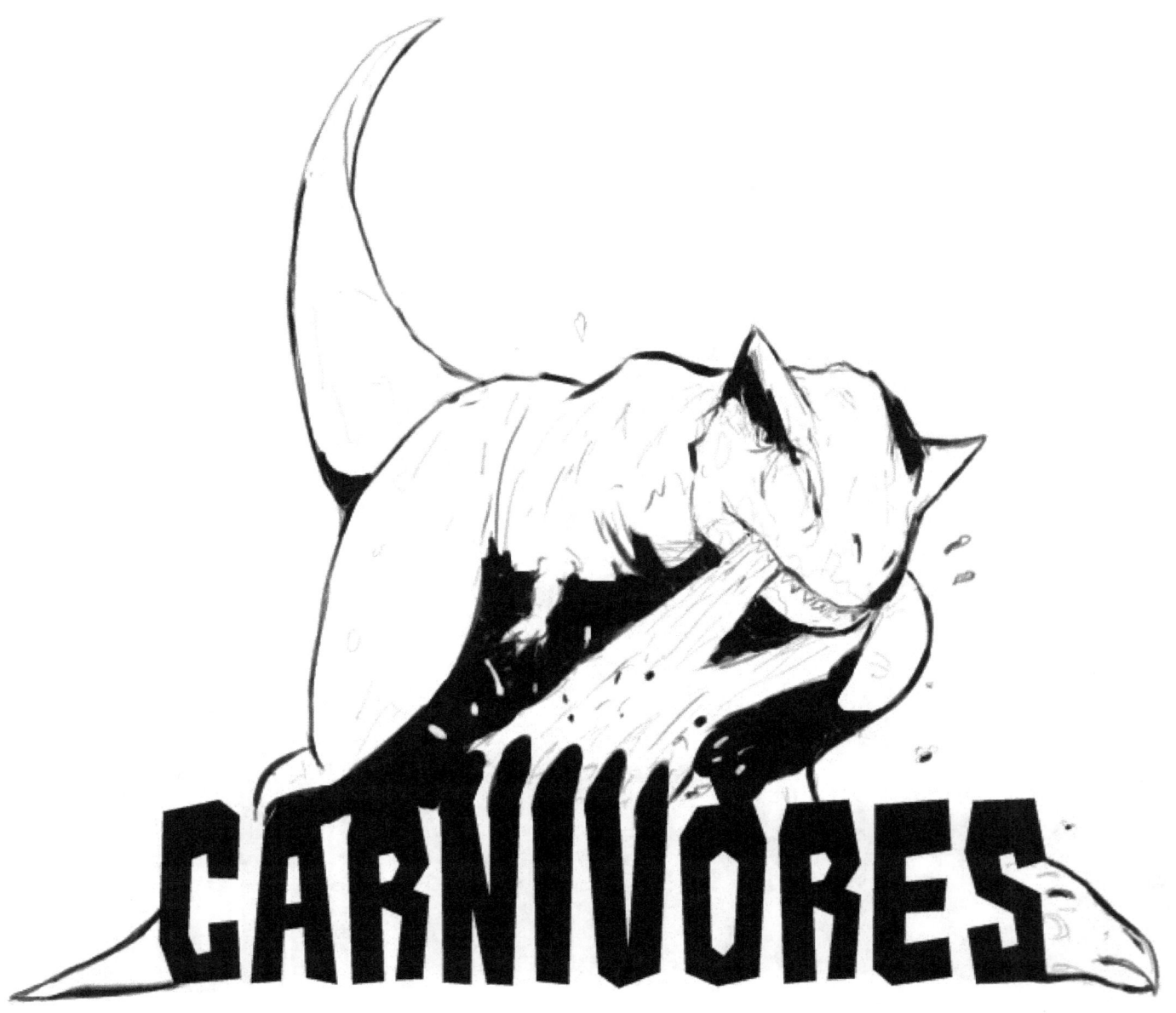

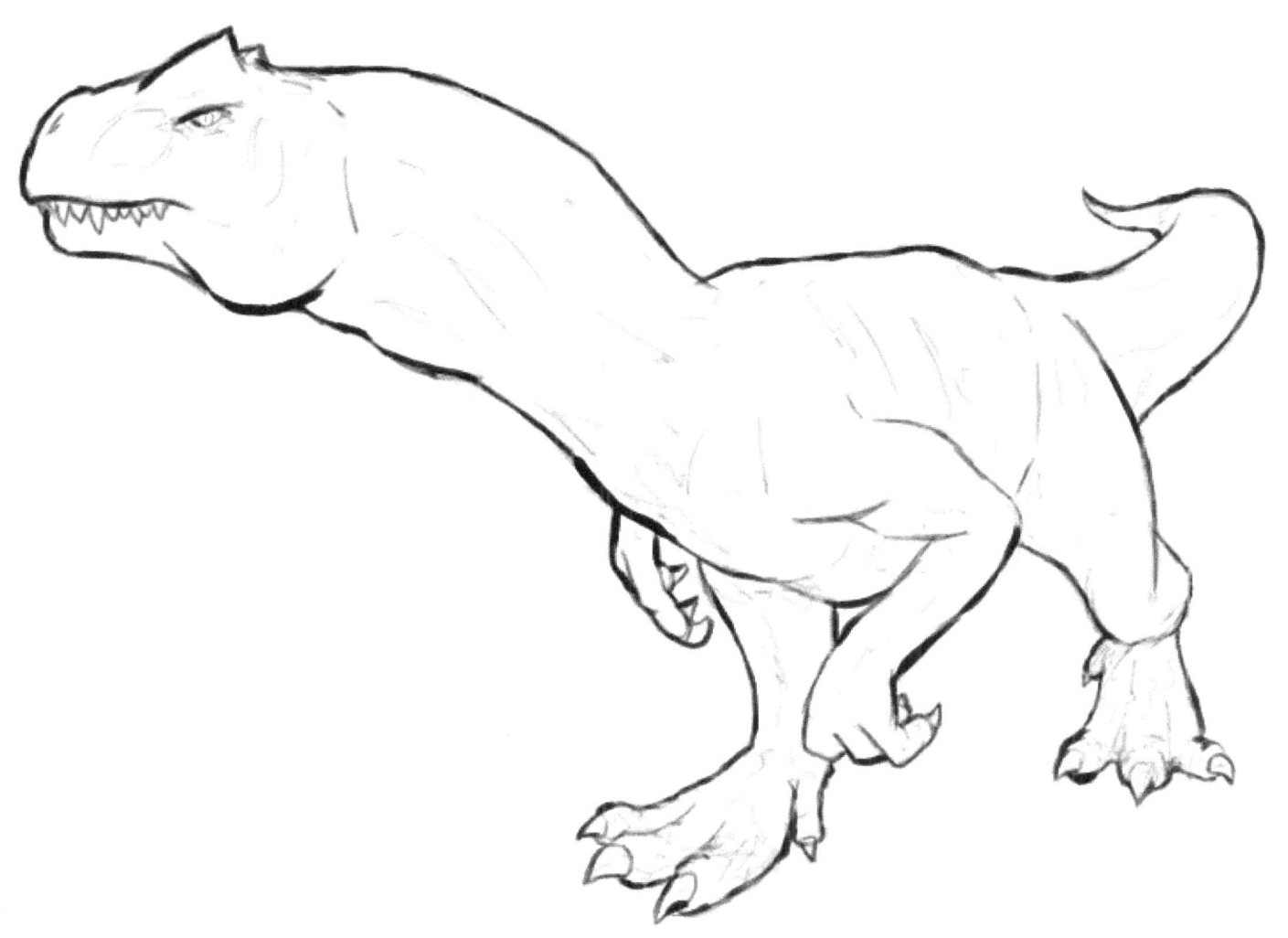

ALLOSAURUS

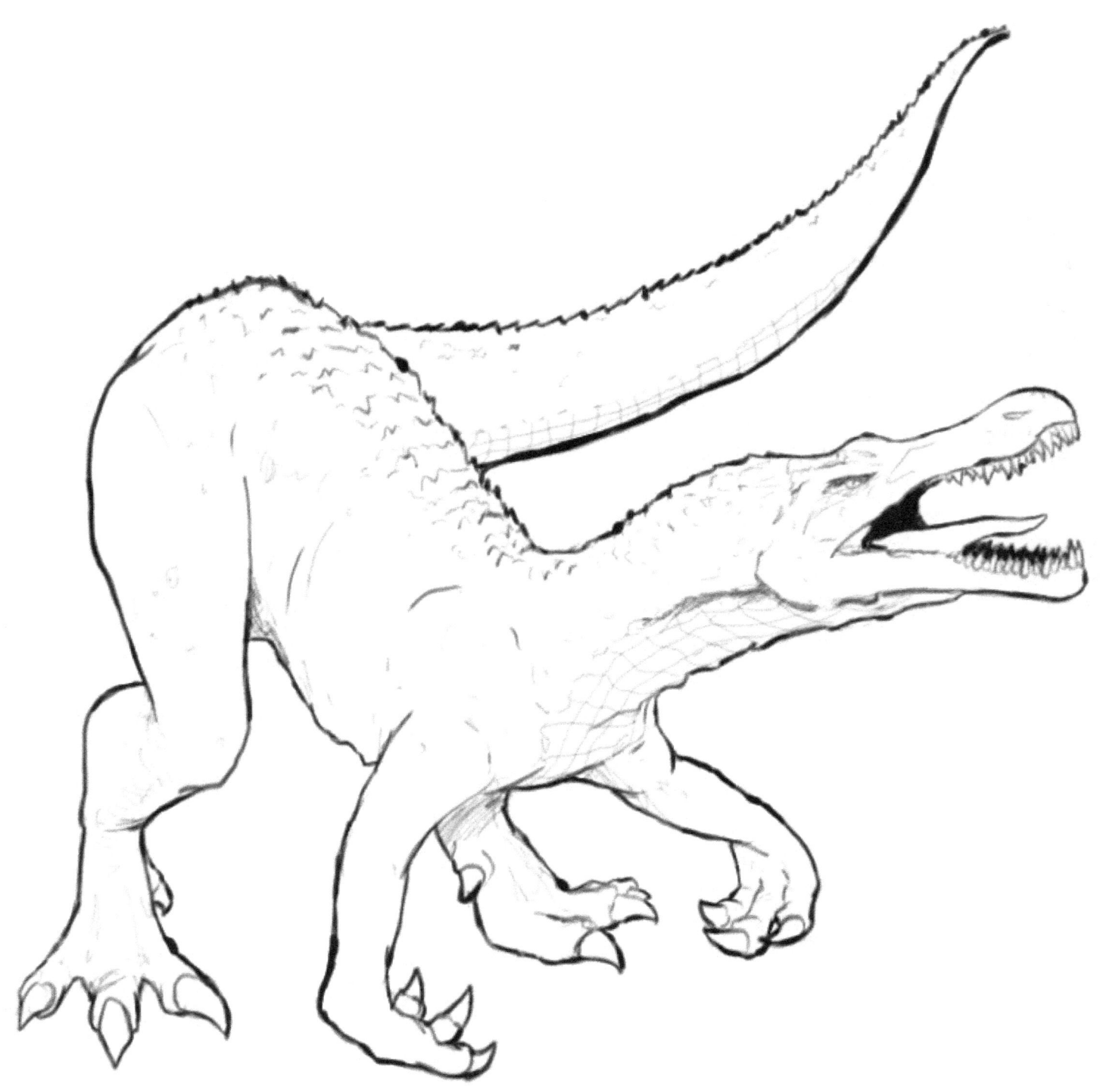

BARYONYX

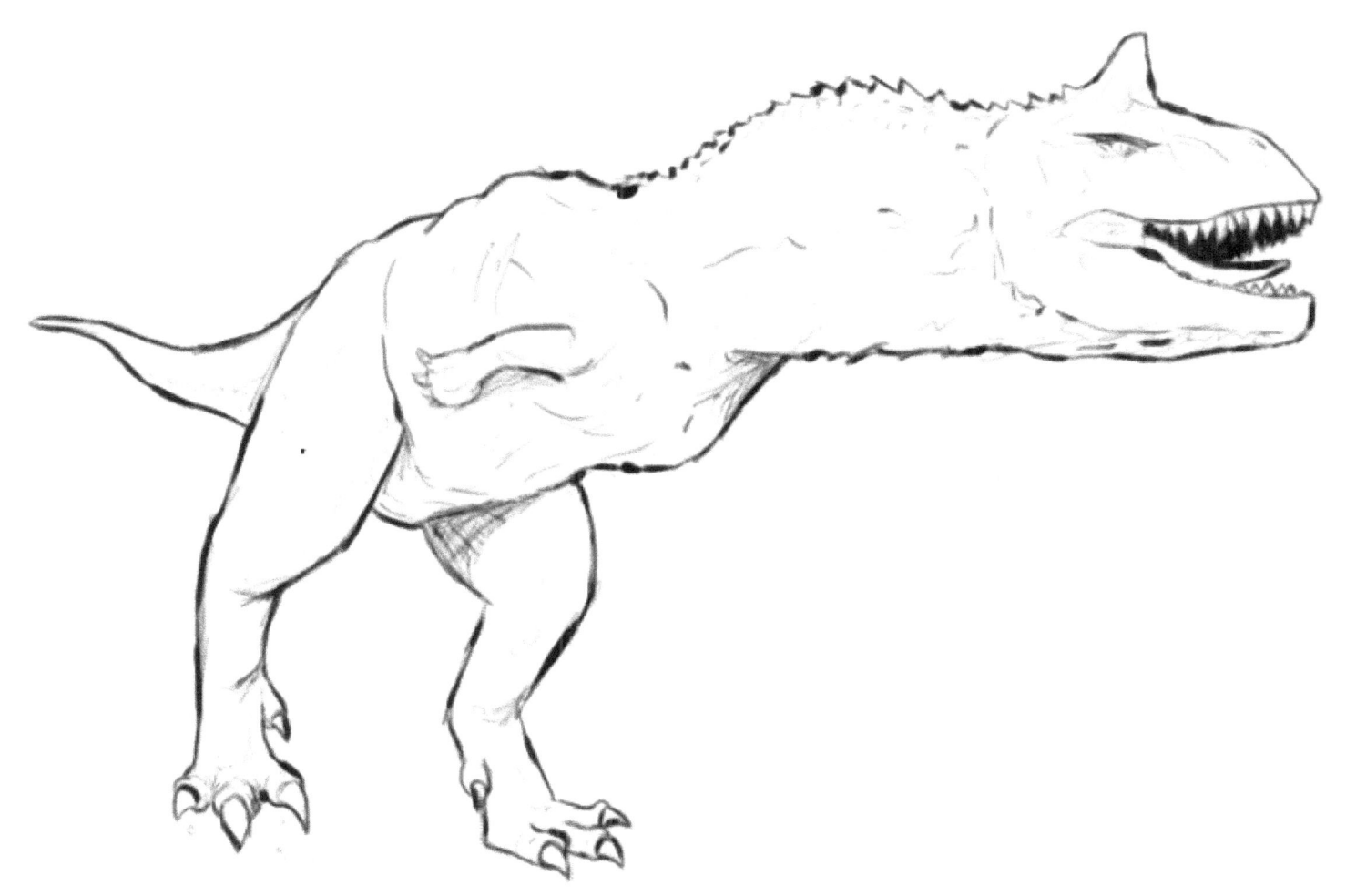

CARNOTAURUS

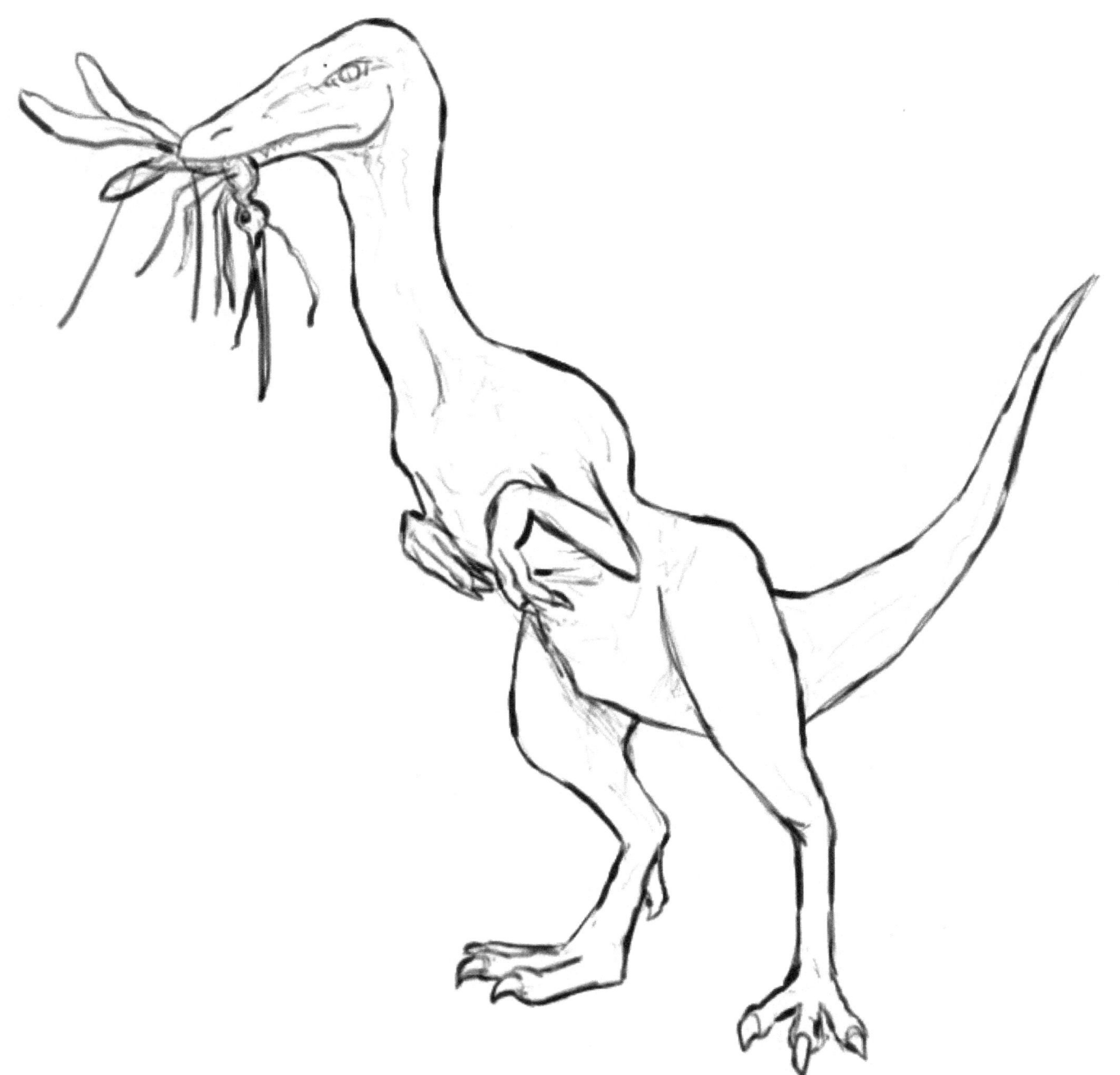

COMPSOGNATHUS

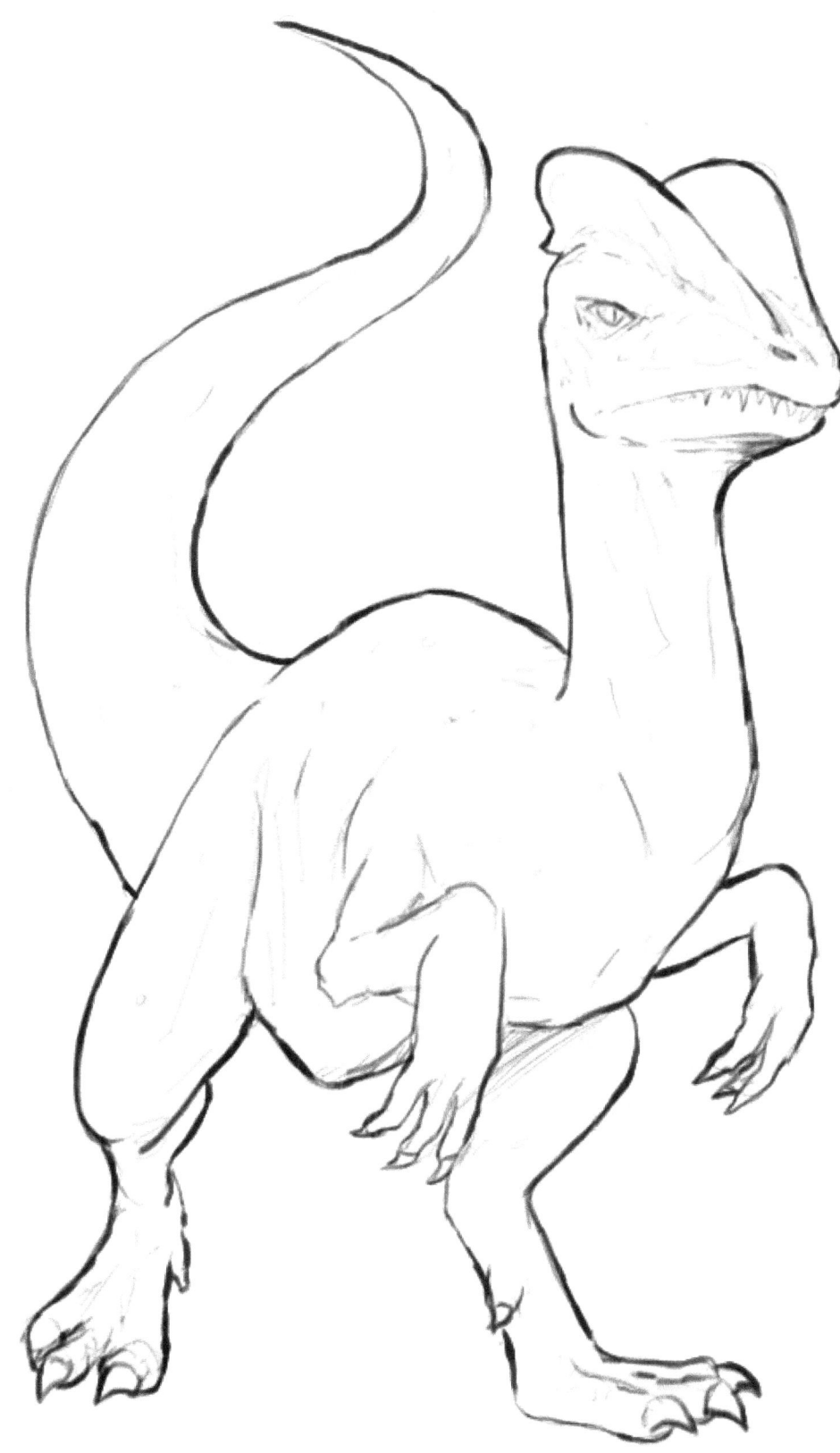

DILOPHOSAURUS

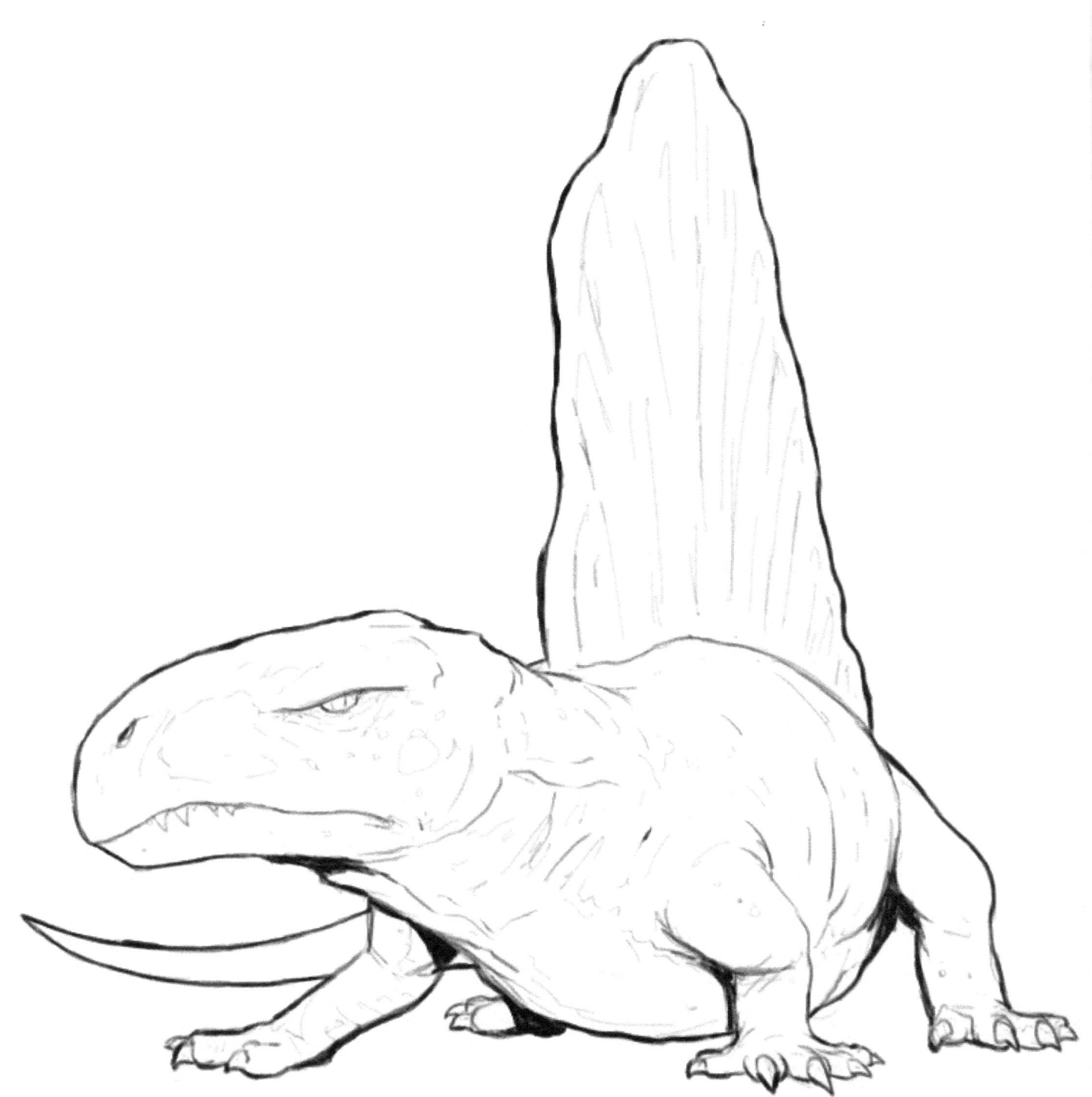

DIMETRODON

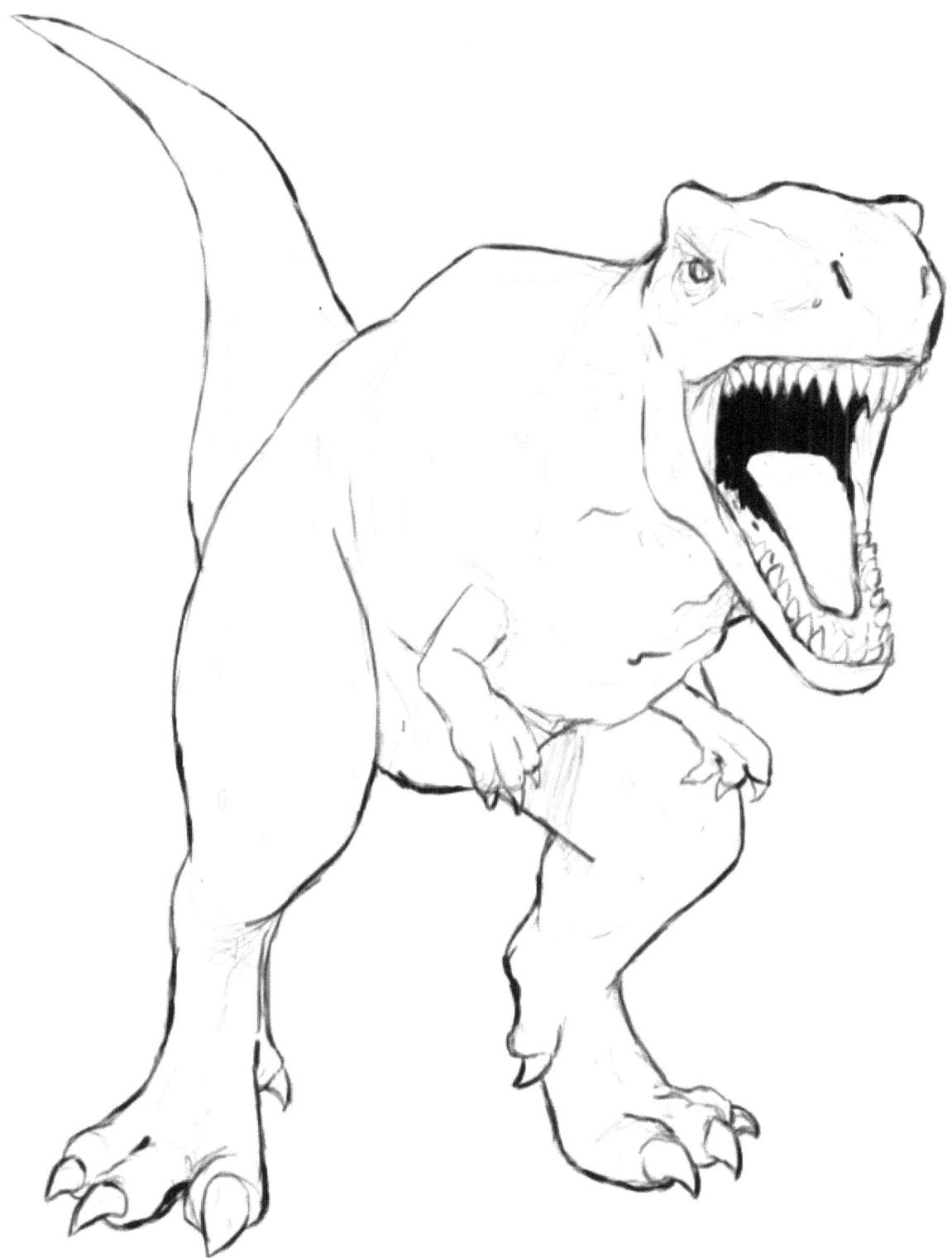

GIGANITOSAURUS

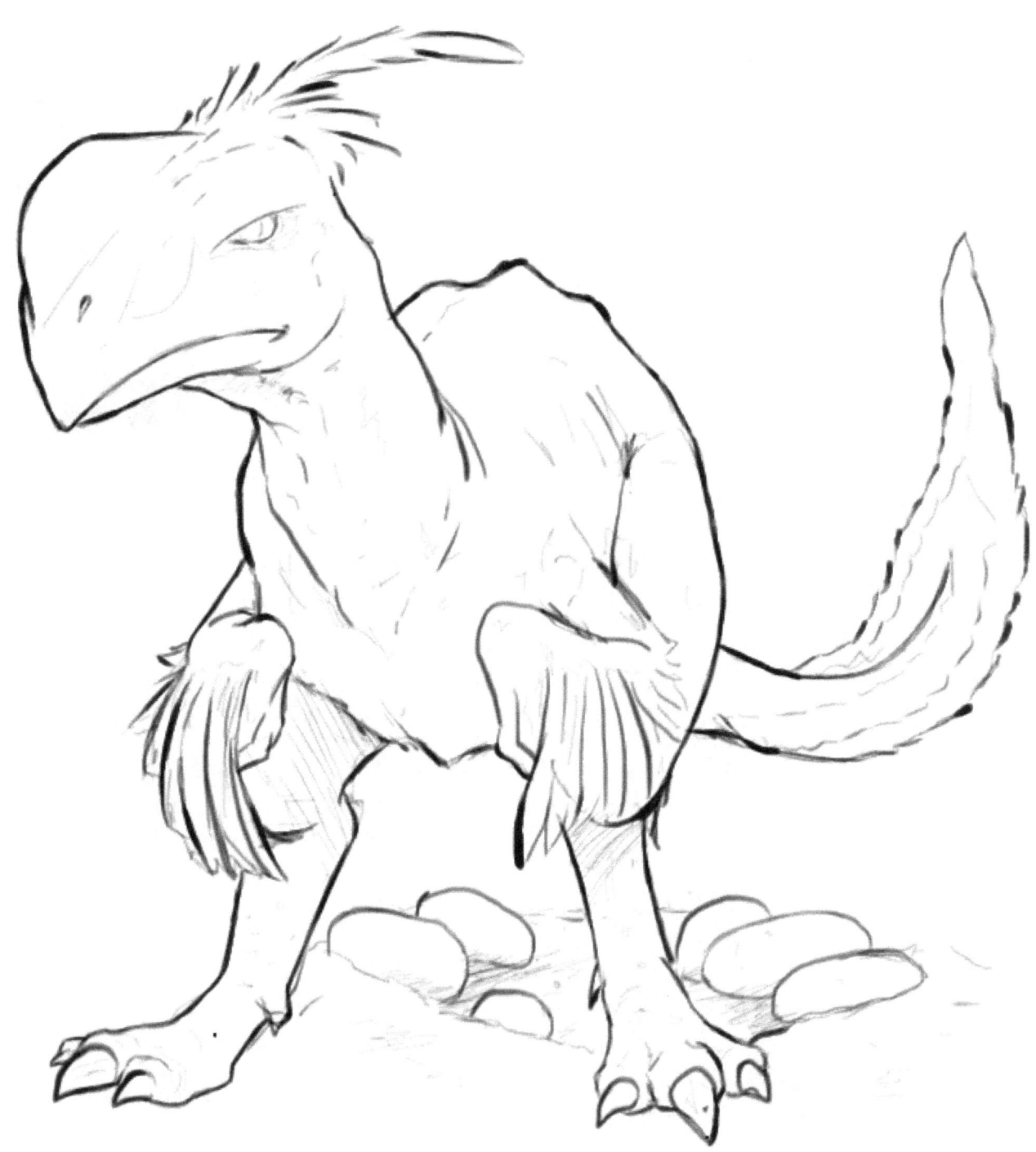

OVIRAPTOR

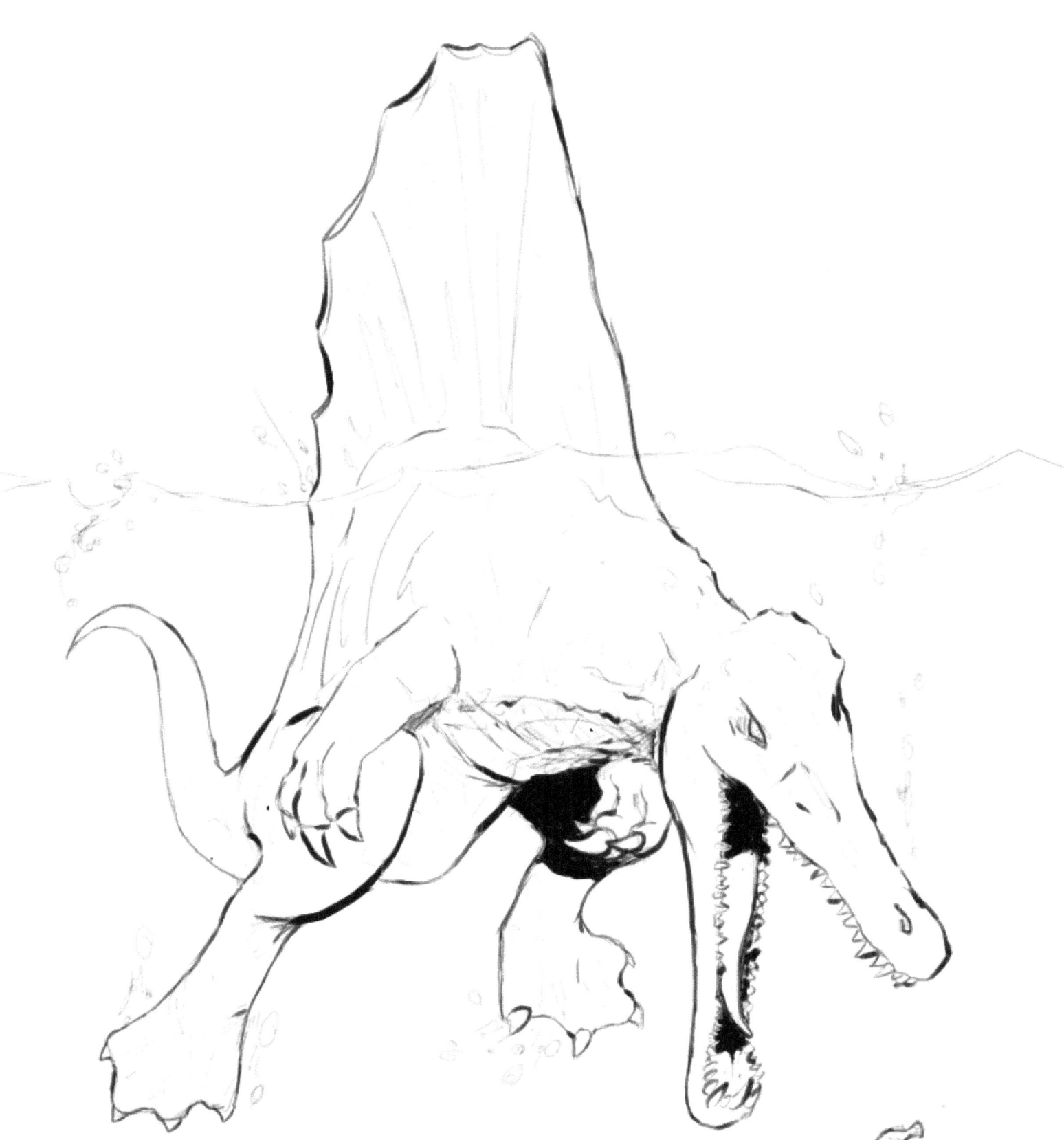

SPINOSAURUS

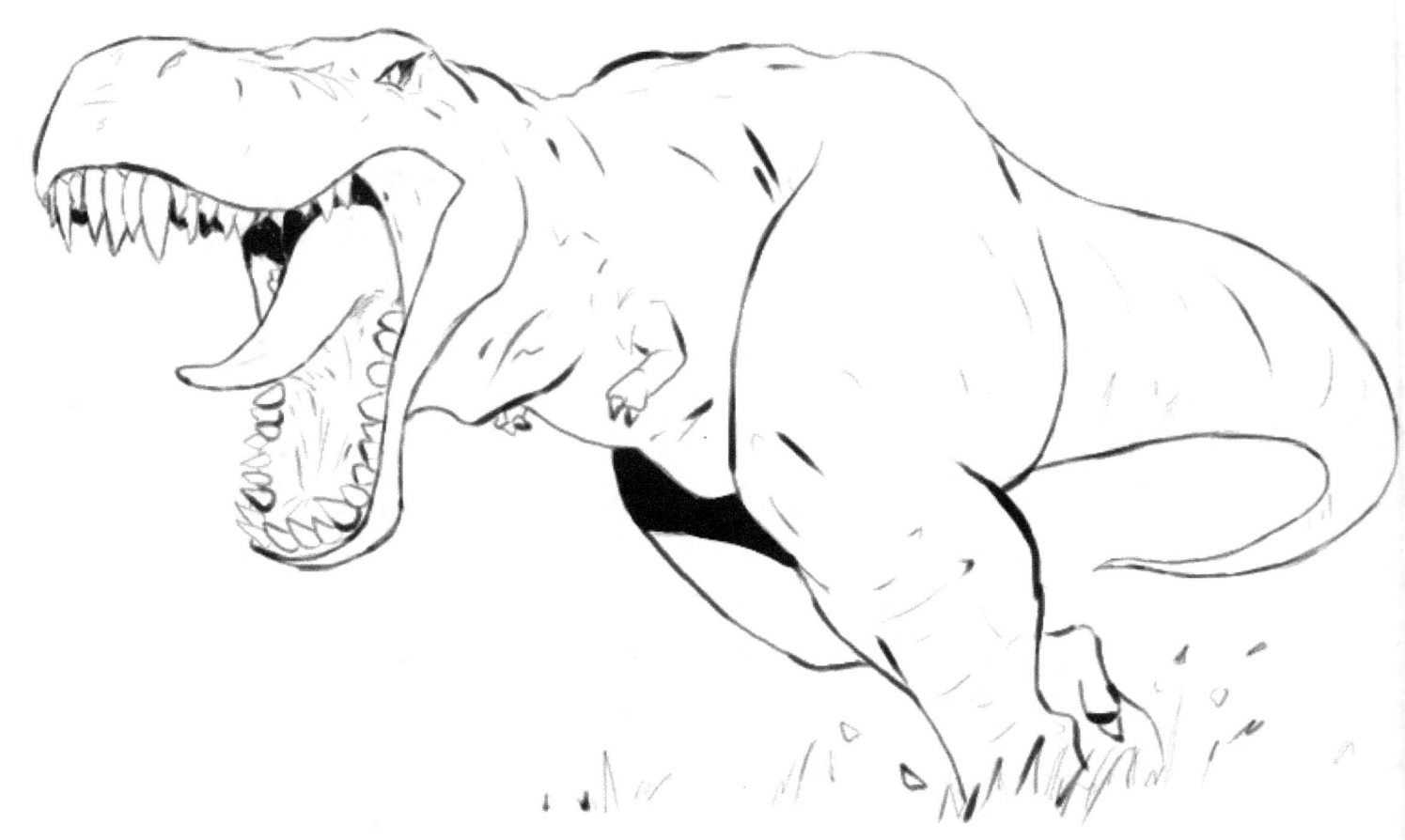

TYRANNOSAURUS REX

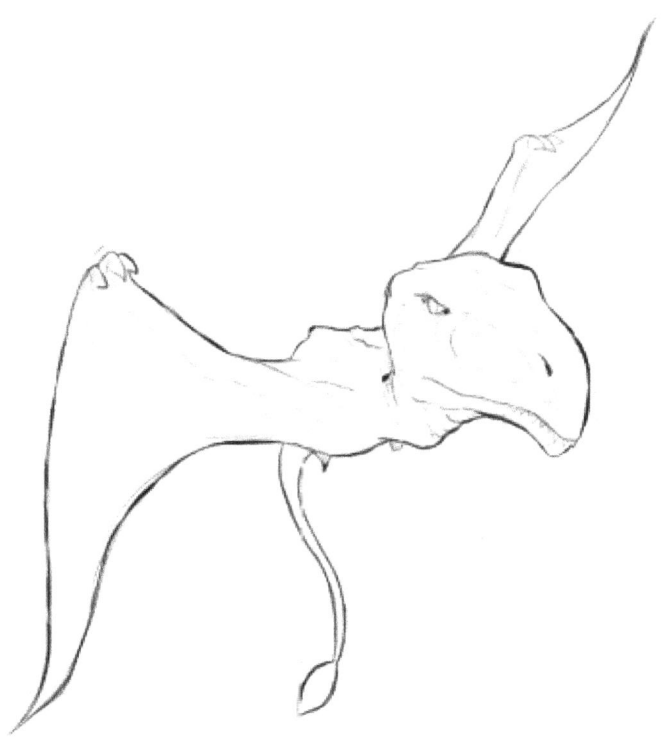

OTHER PREHISTORIC BEASTS

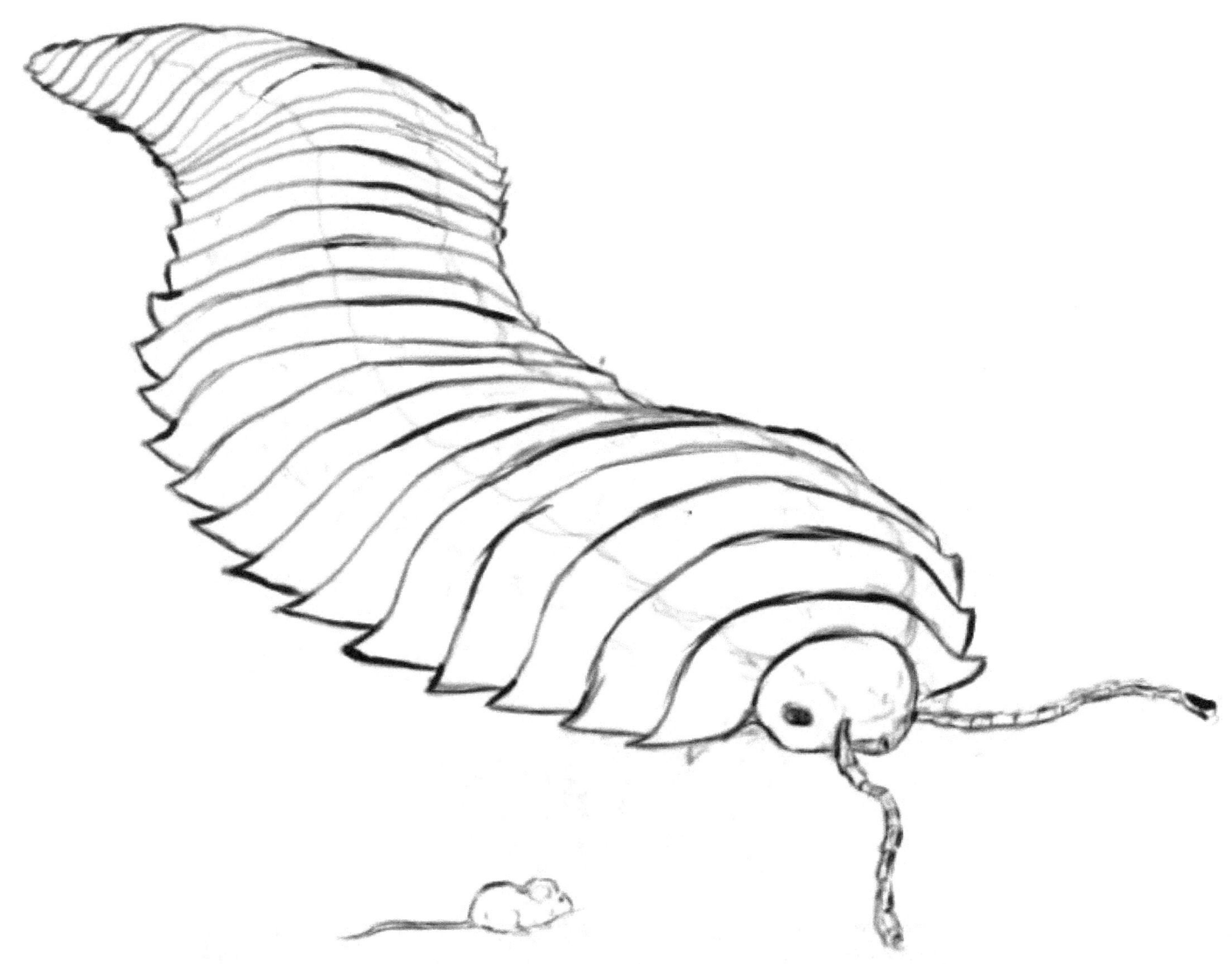

ANTHROPLEURA

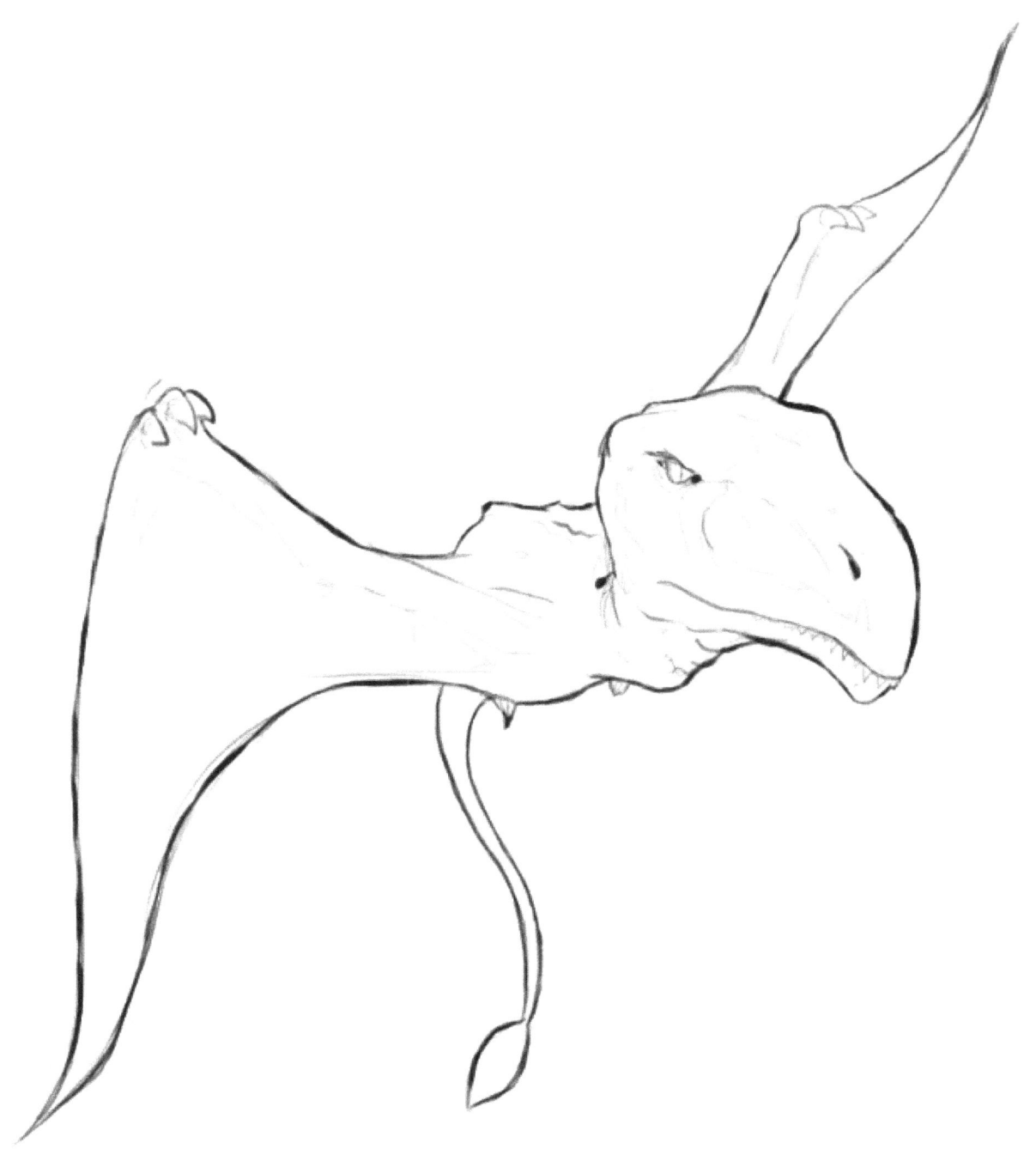

DIMORPHODON

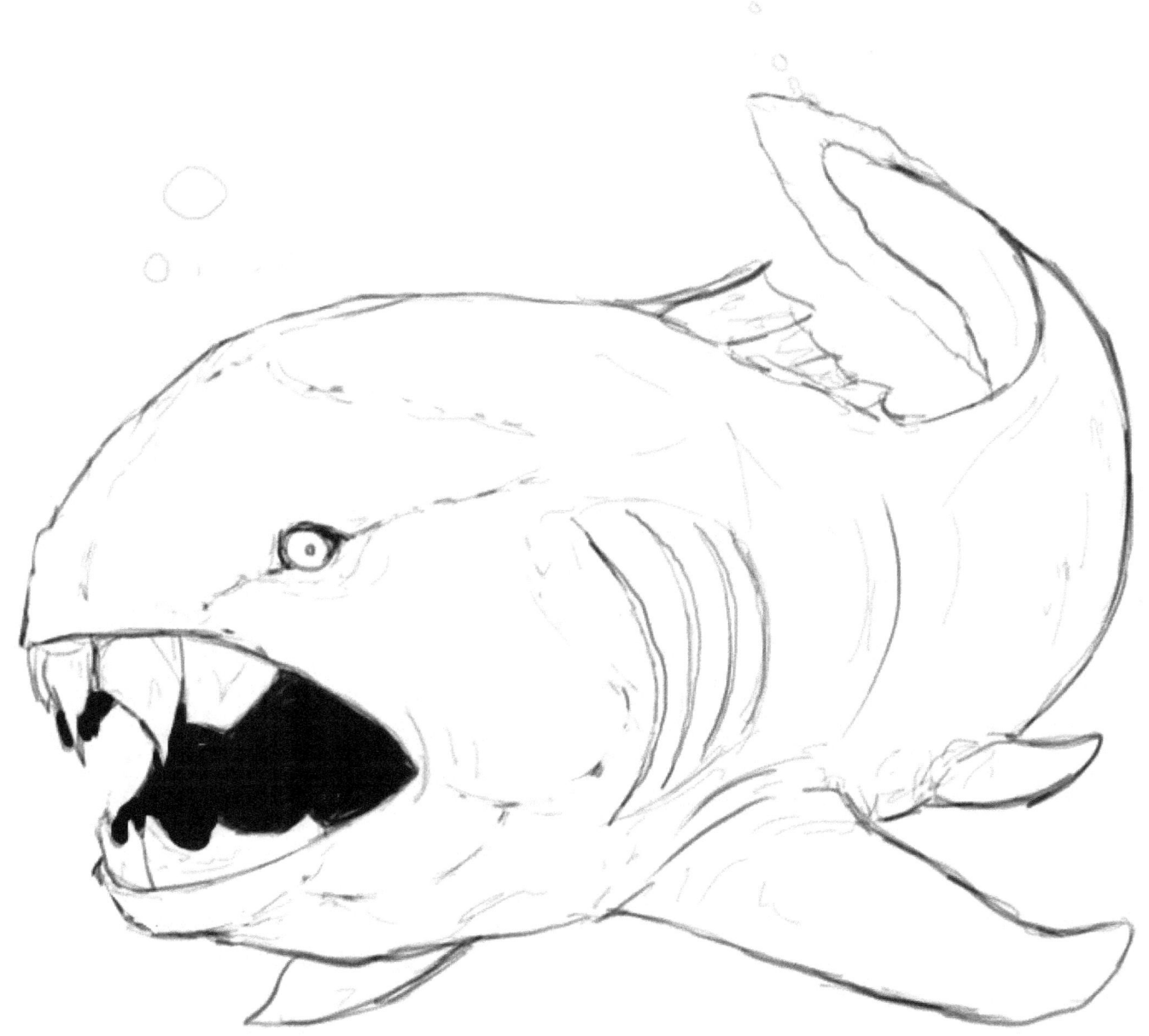

DUNKLEOSTEUS

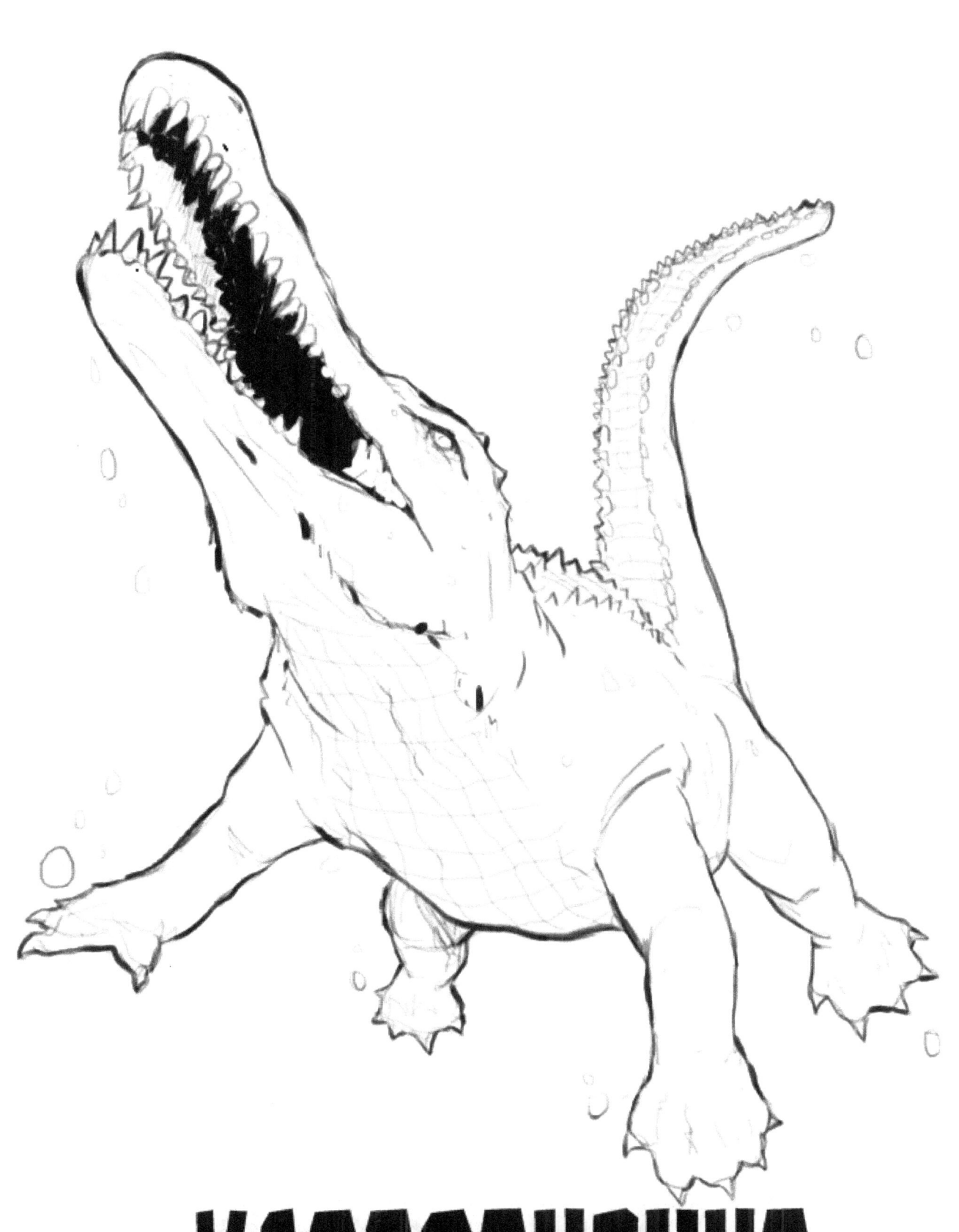

KAPROSUCHUS

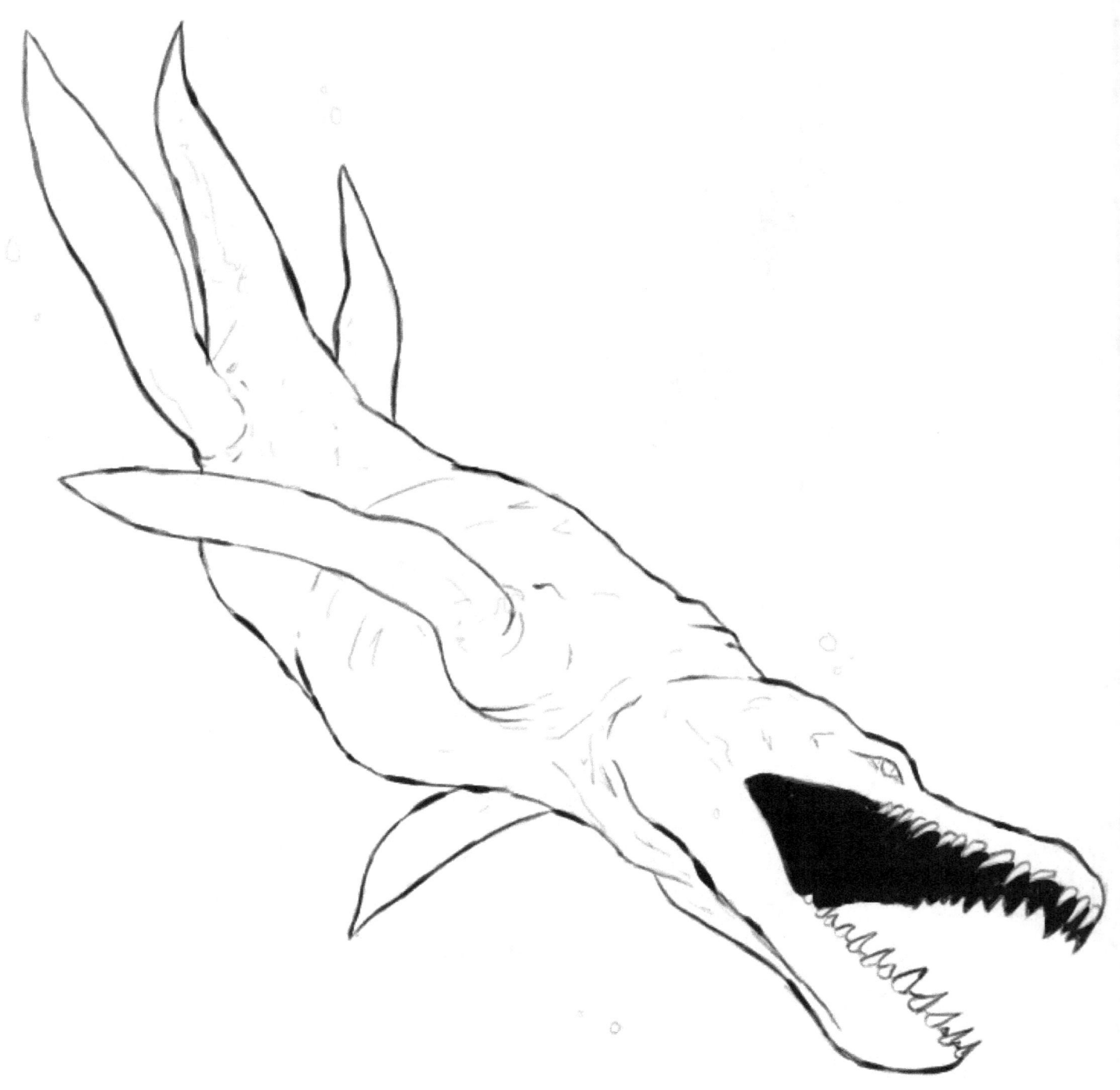

LIOPLEURODON

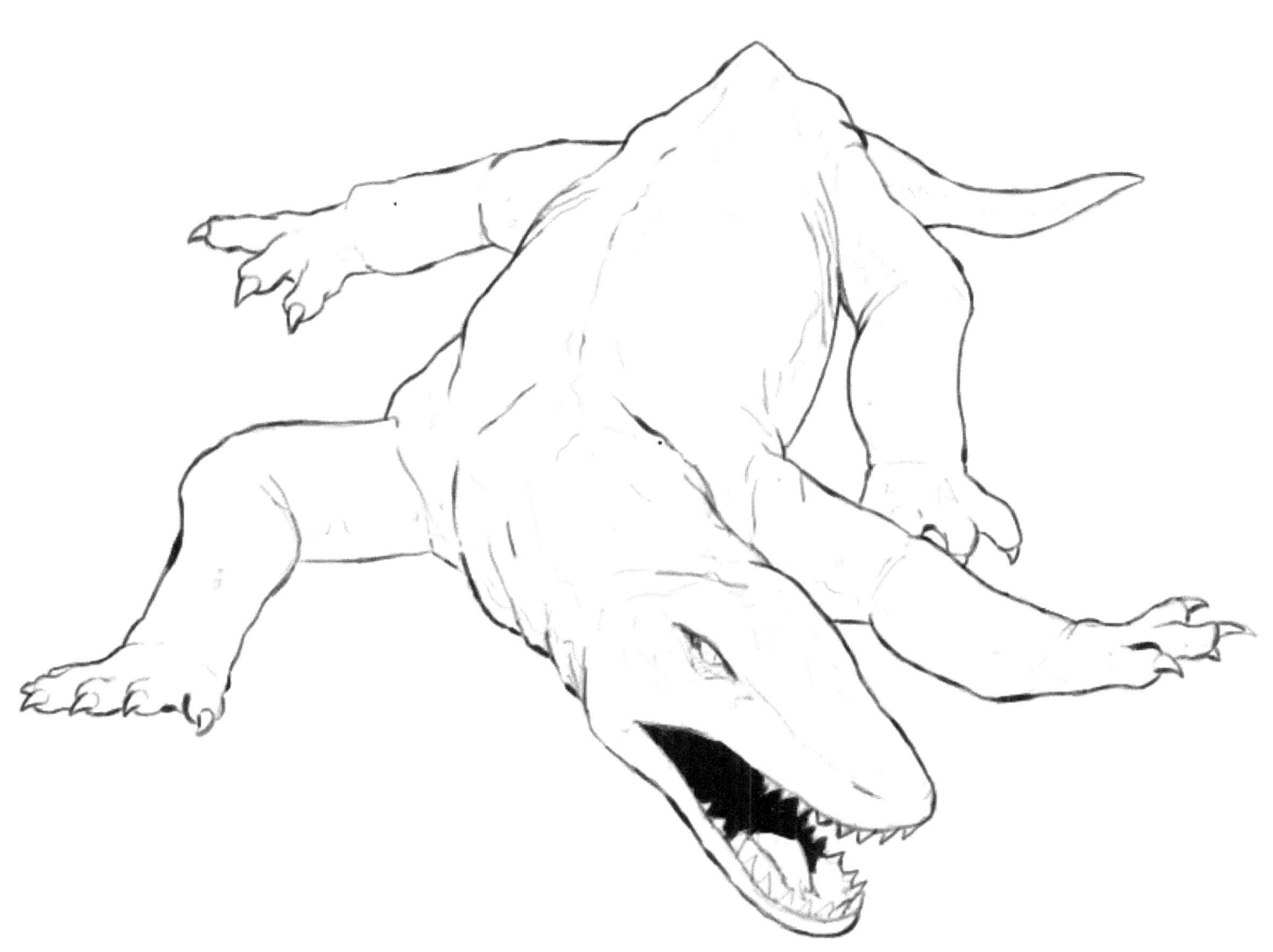

MEGALANIA

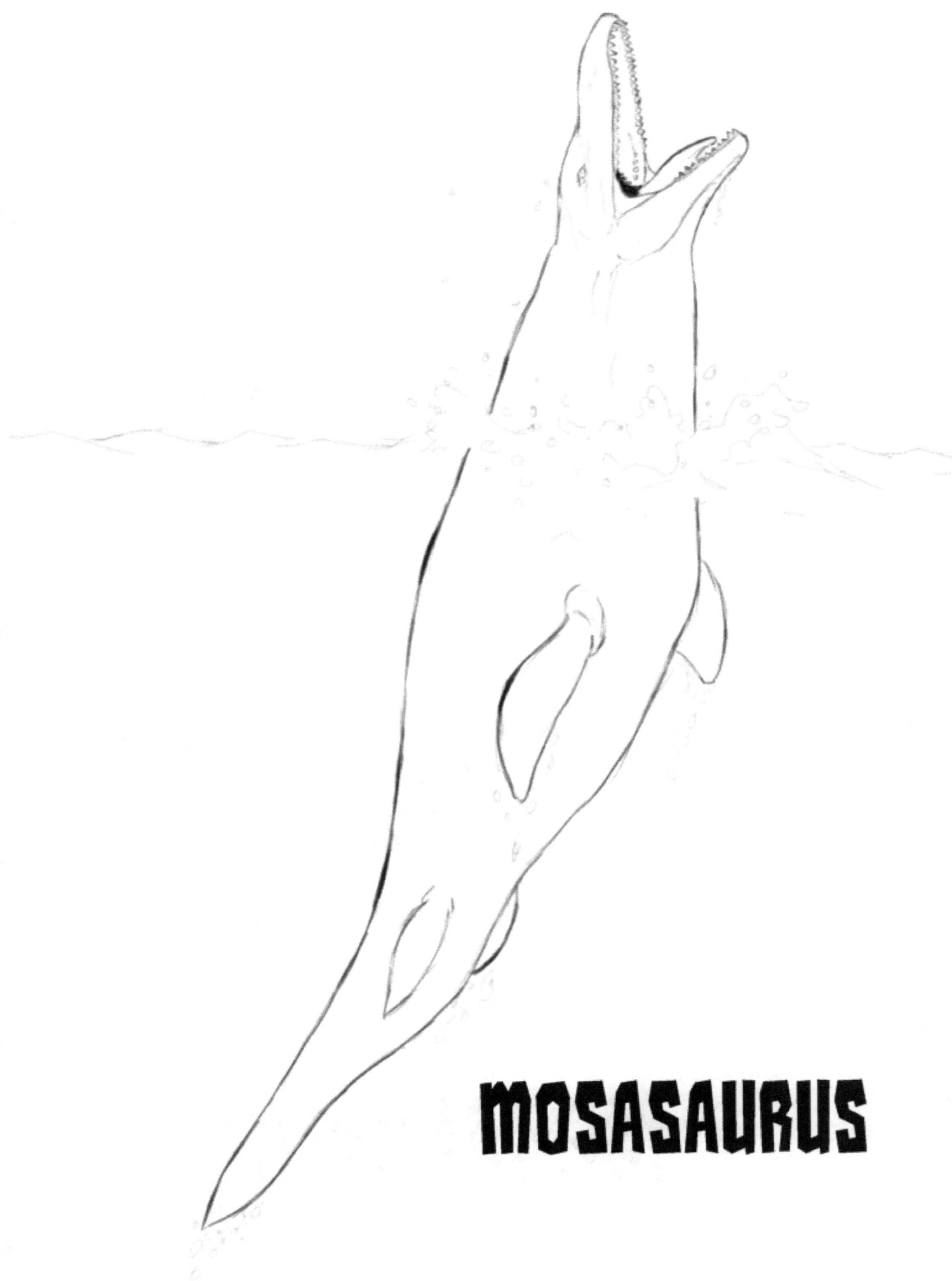

MOSASAURUS

PTERANODON

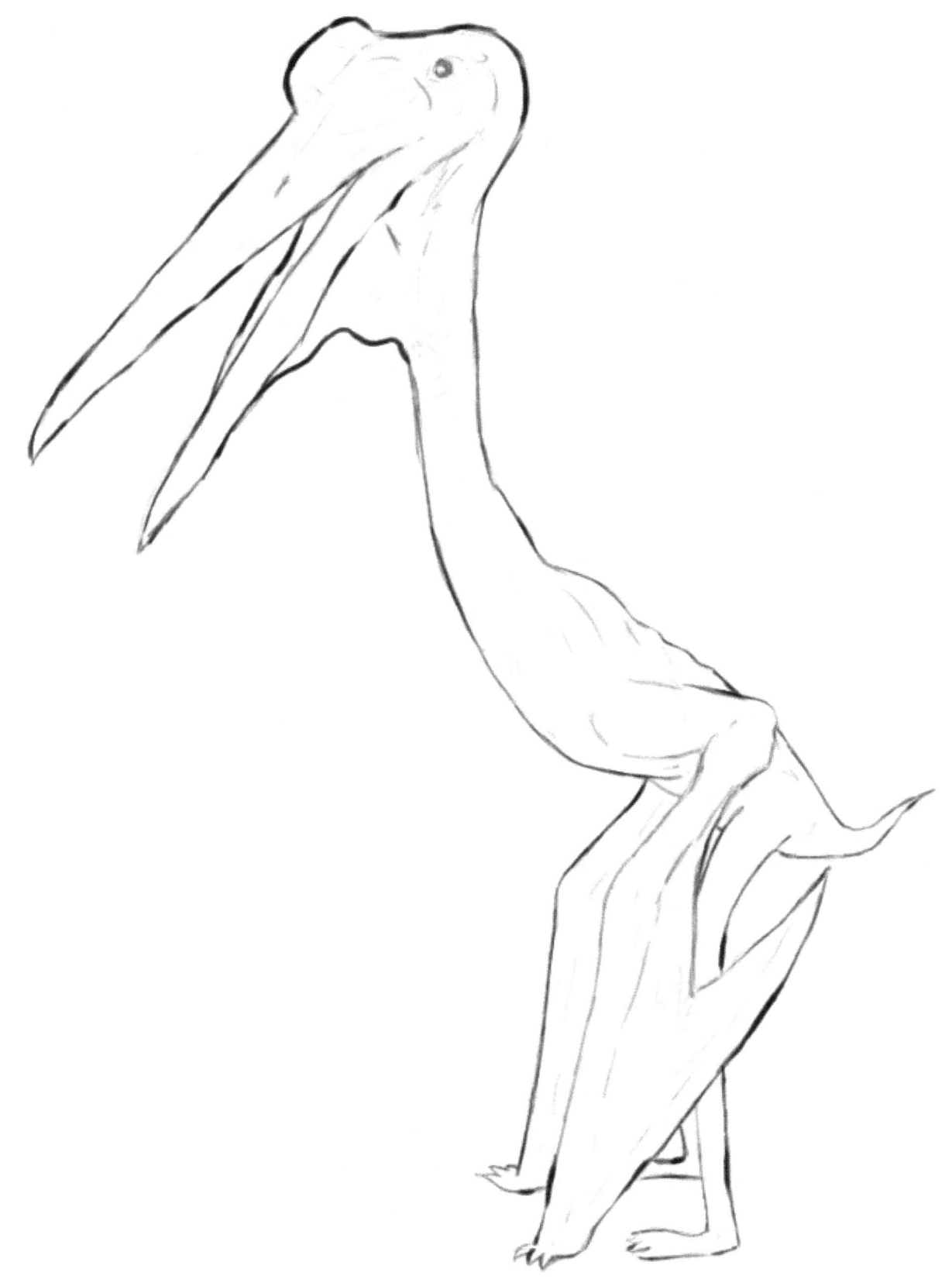

QEUTZALCOATLUS

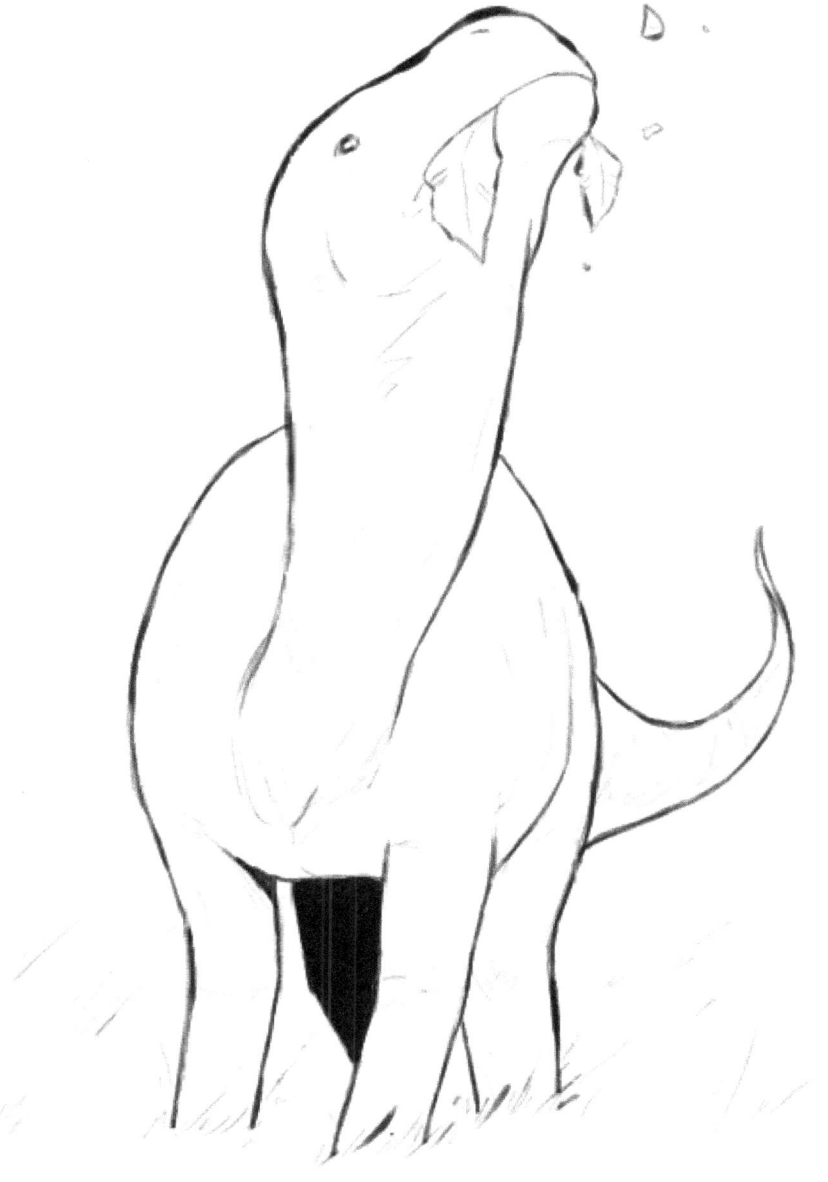

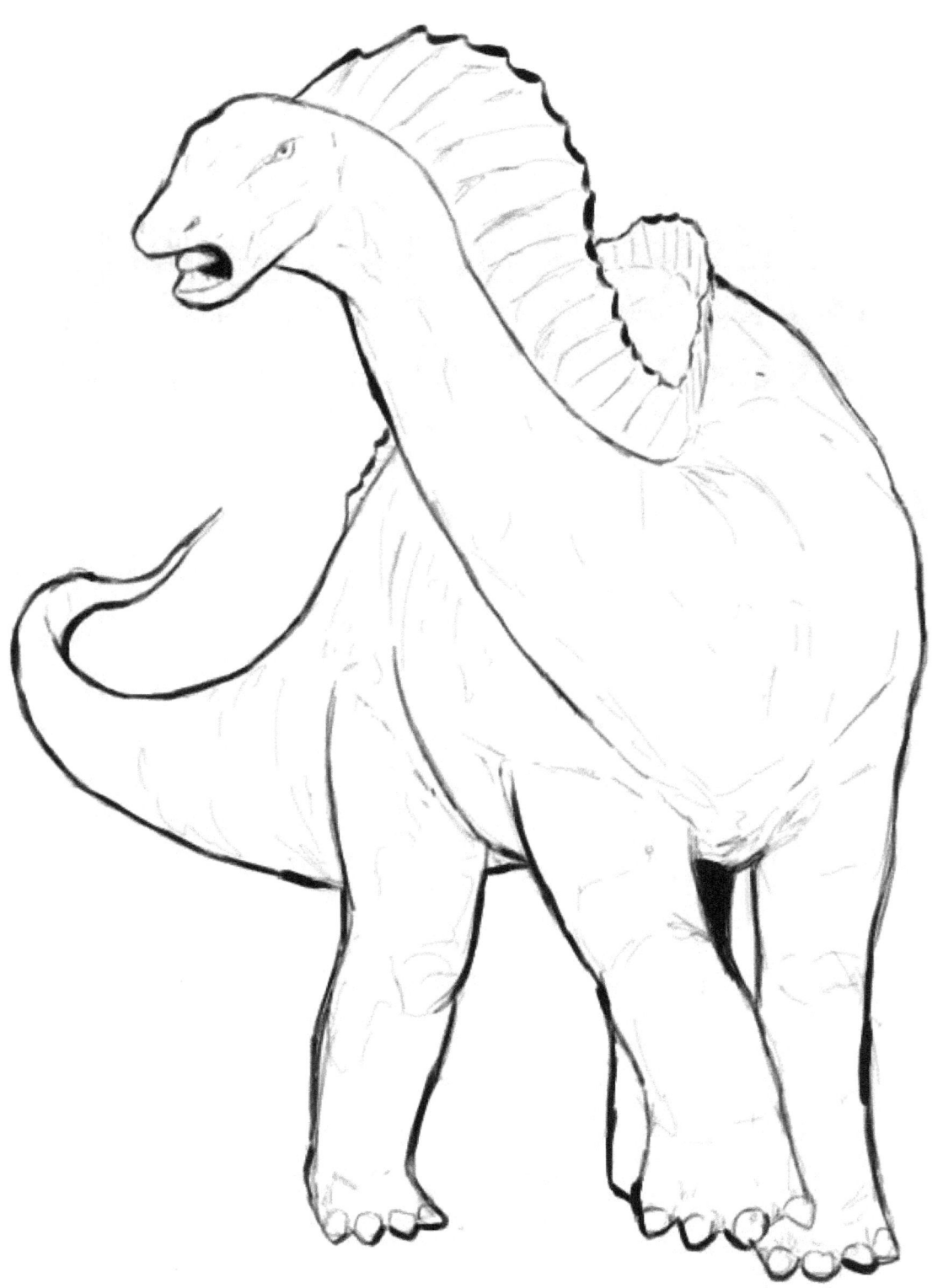

AMARGASAURUS

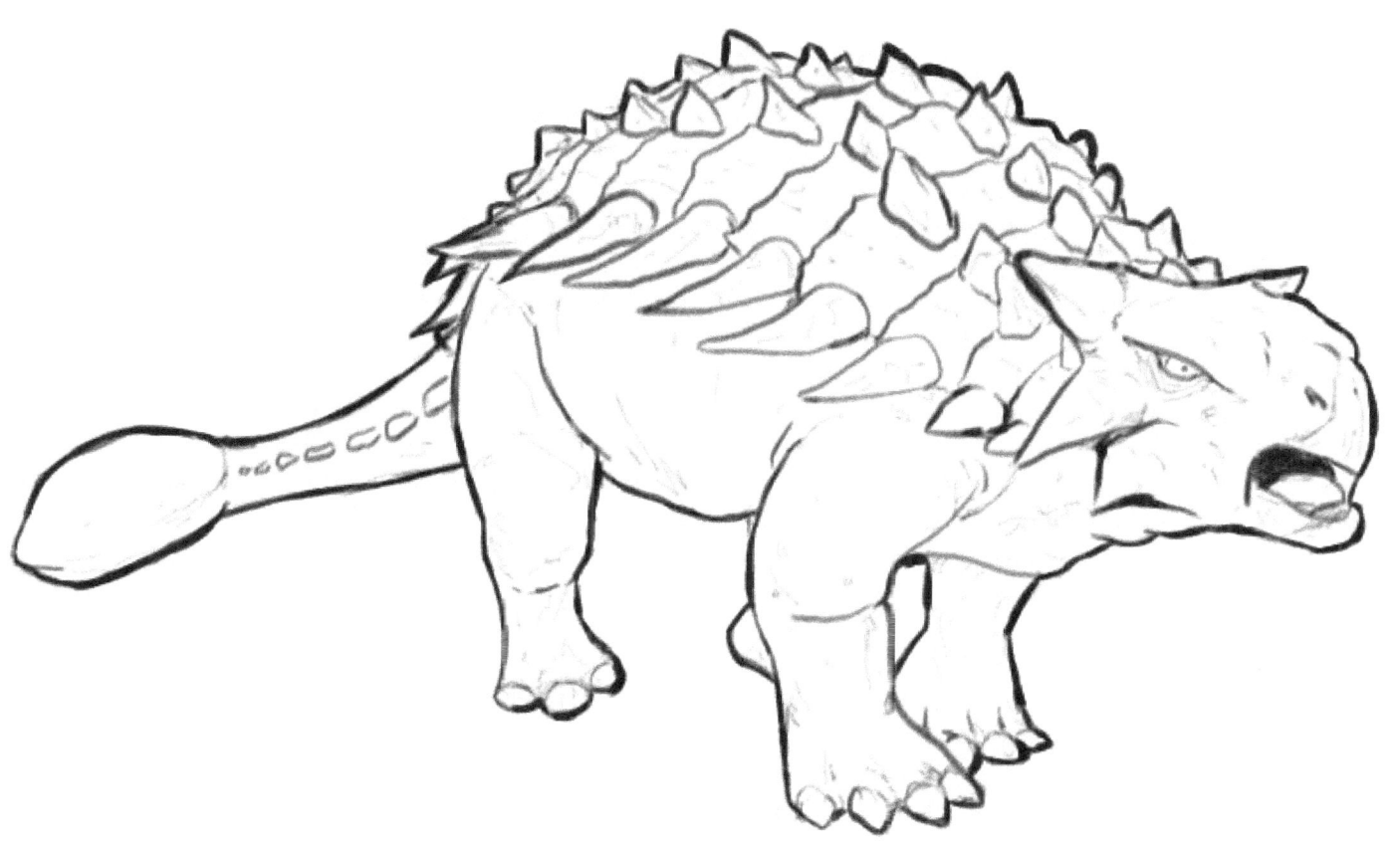

ANKYLOSAURUS

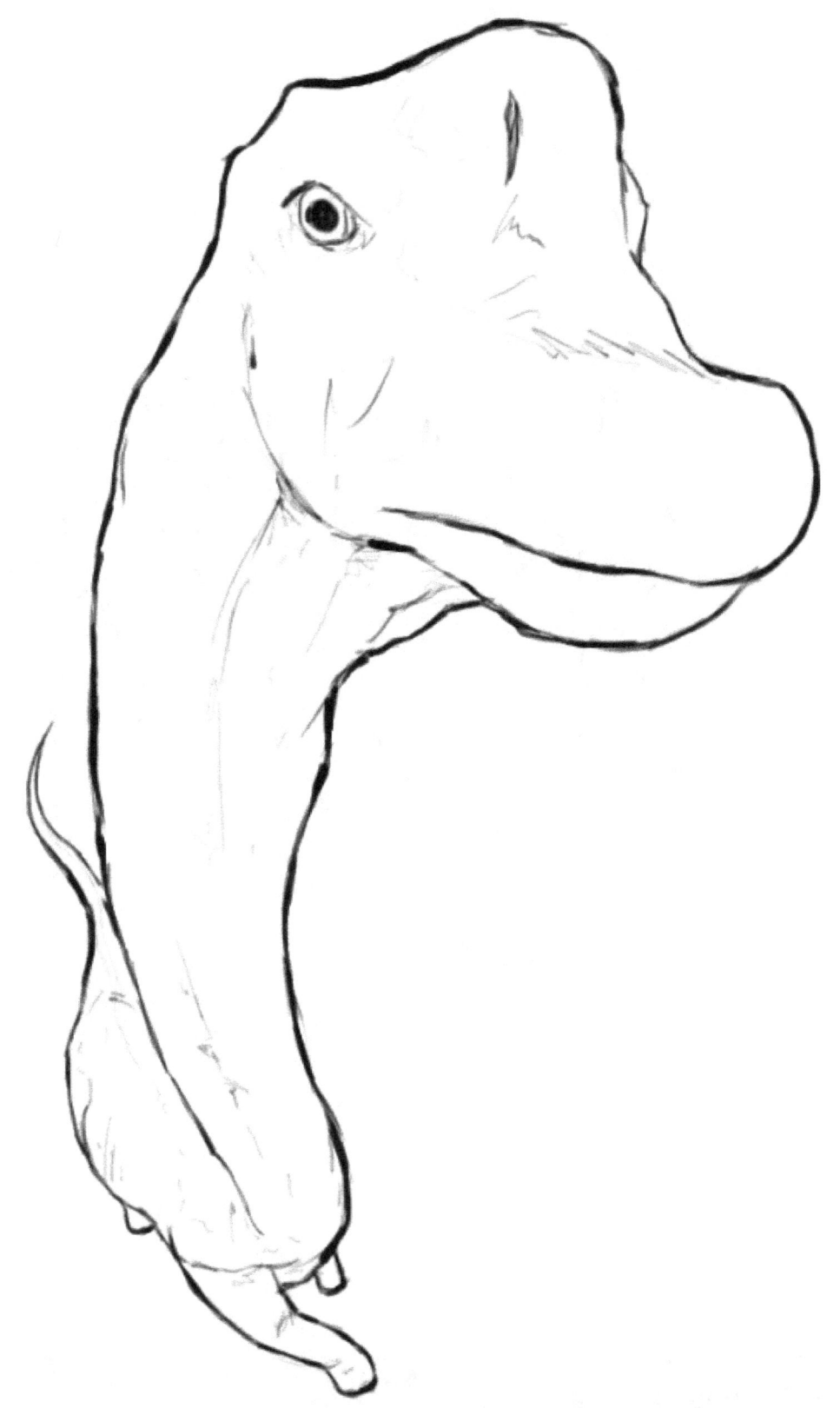

BRACHIOSAURUS

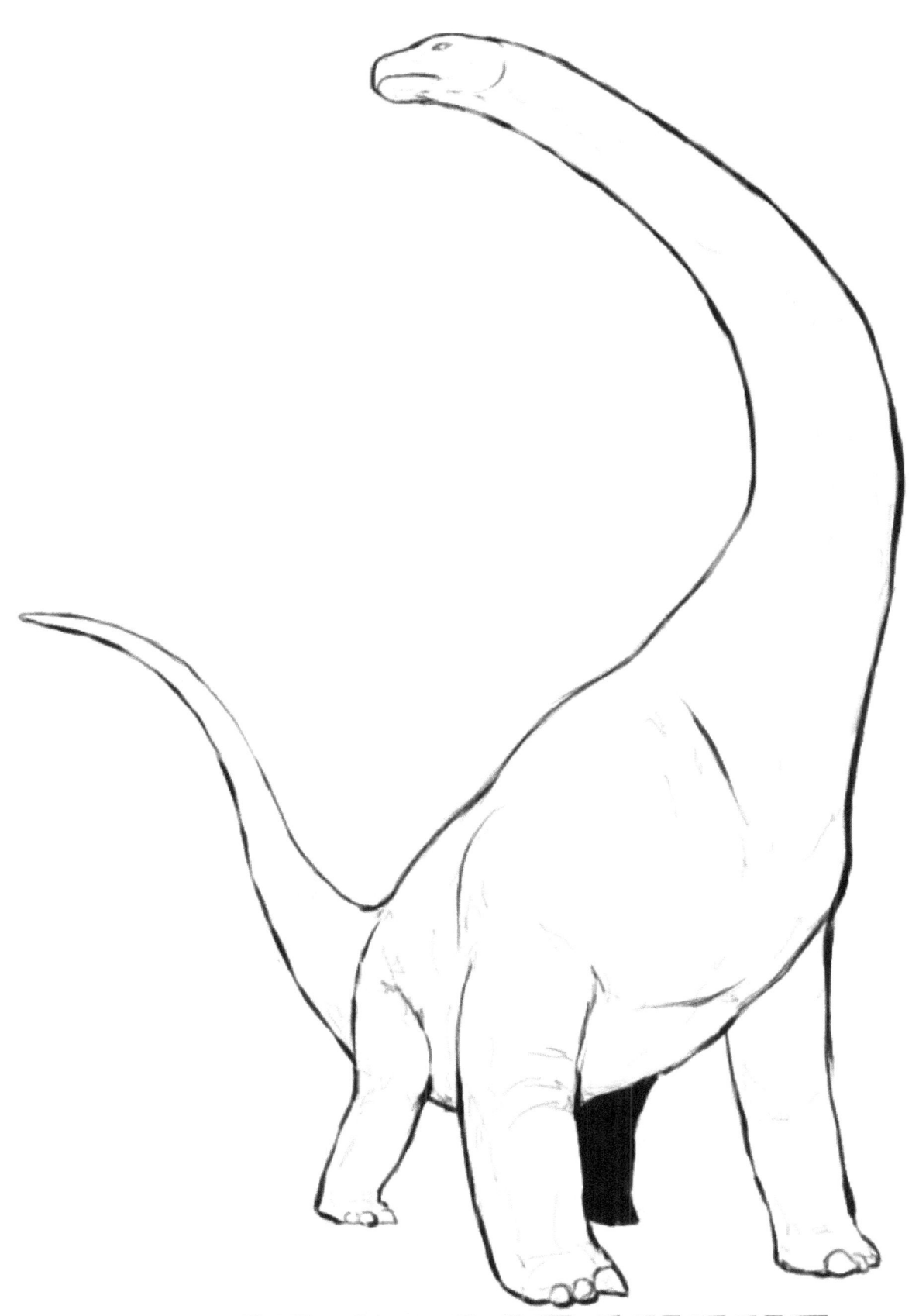

BRONTOSAURUS
(aka Apatosaurus)

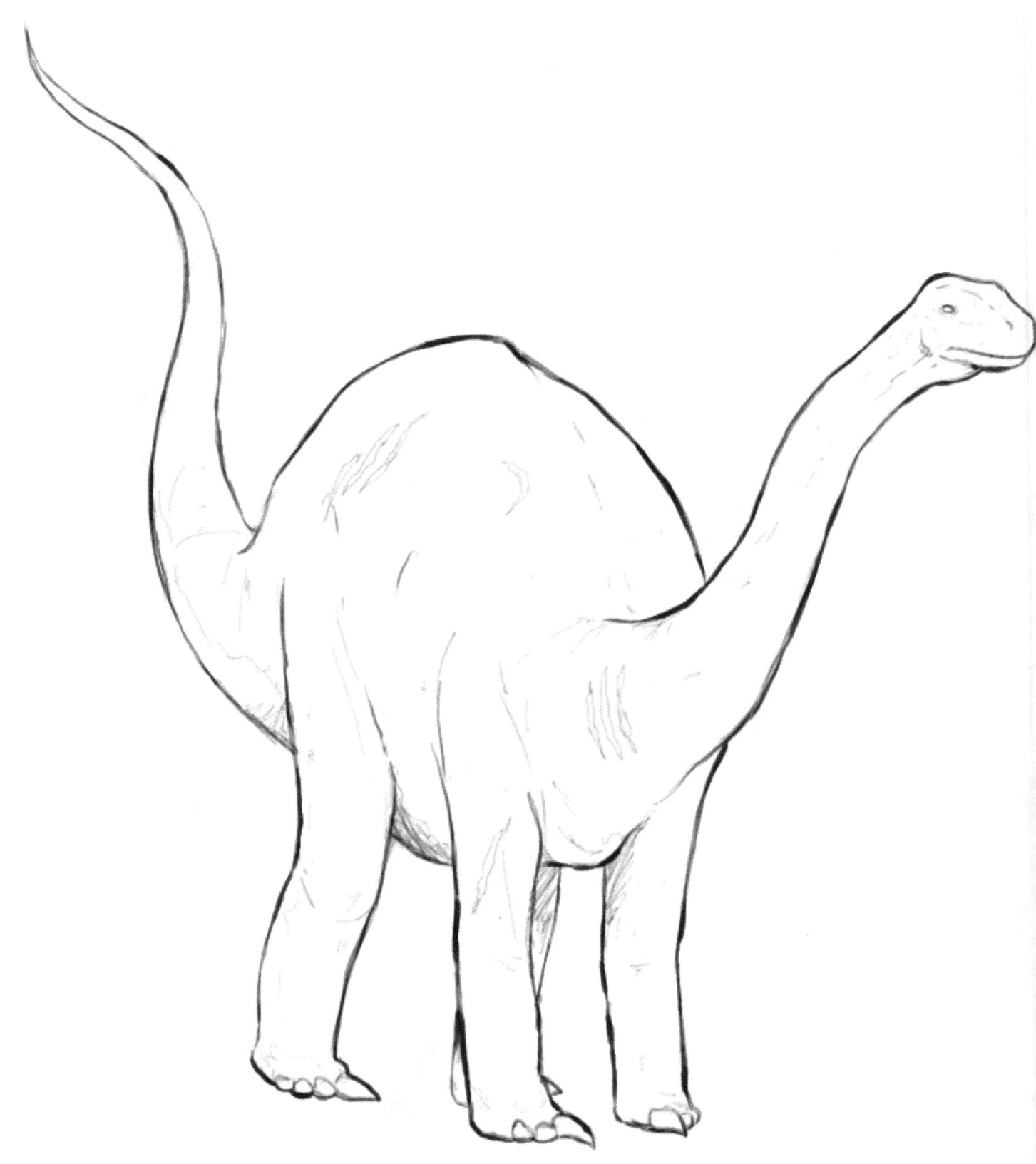

DIPLODOCUS

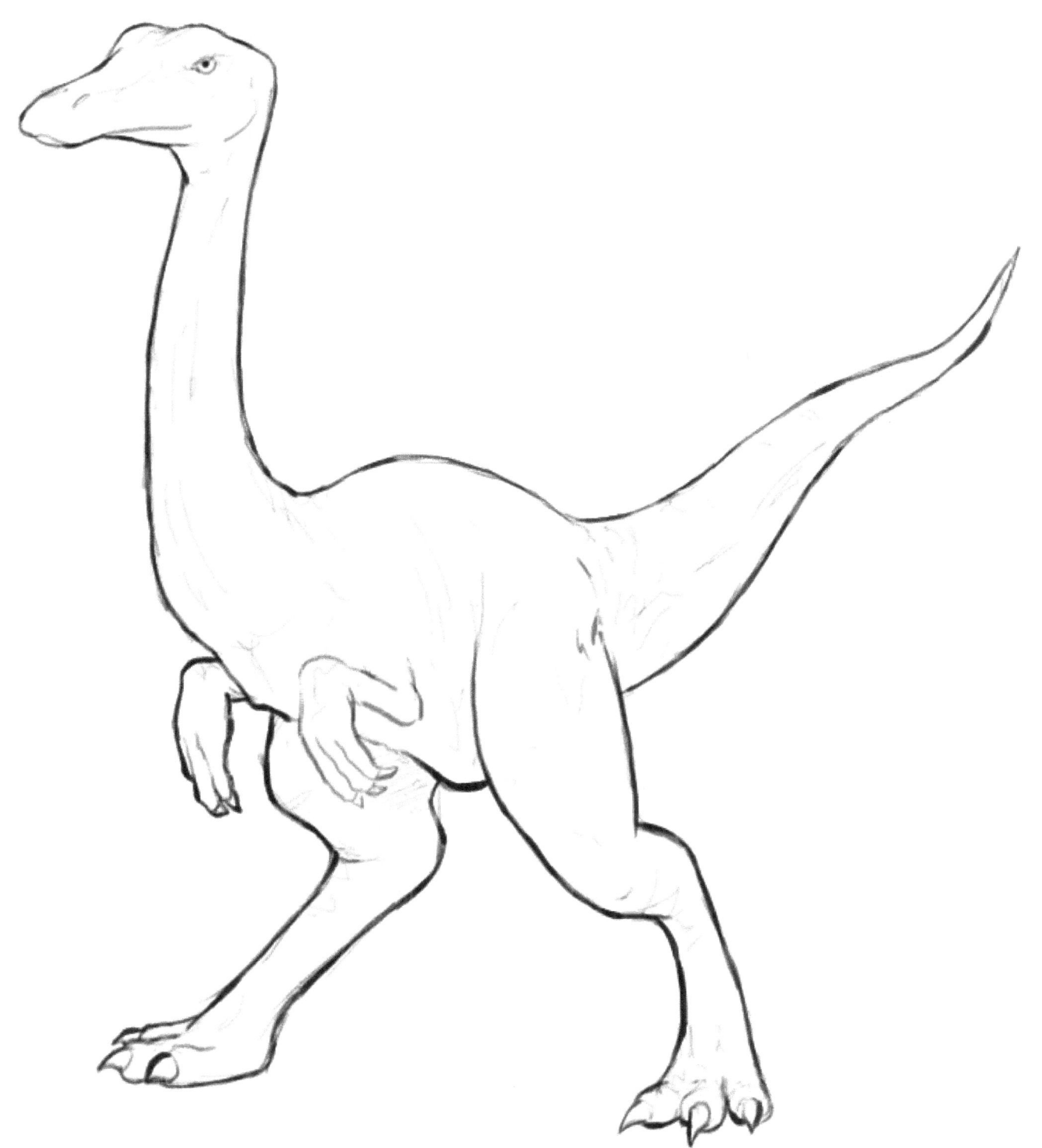

GALLIMIMUS

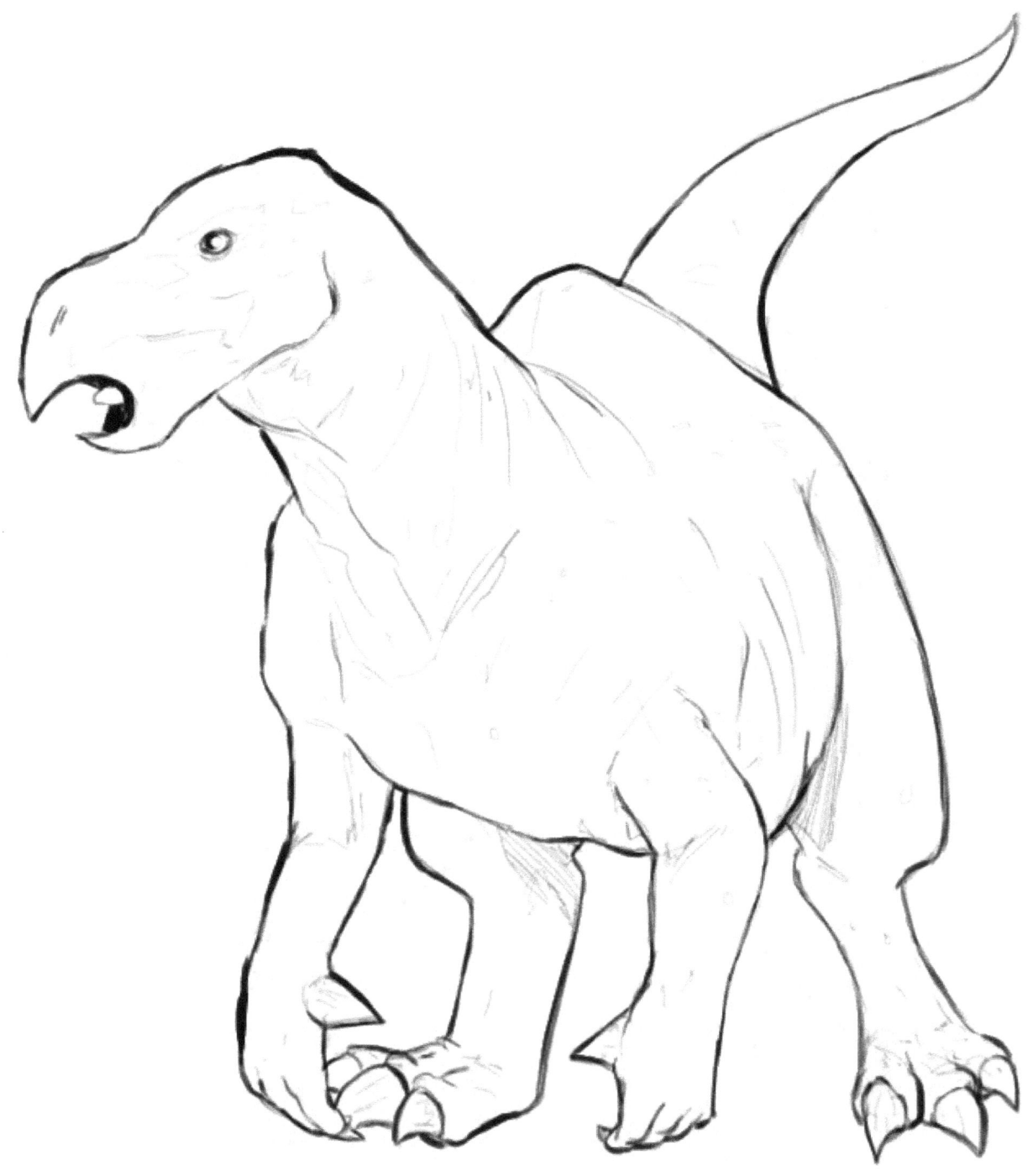

IGUANADON

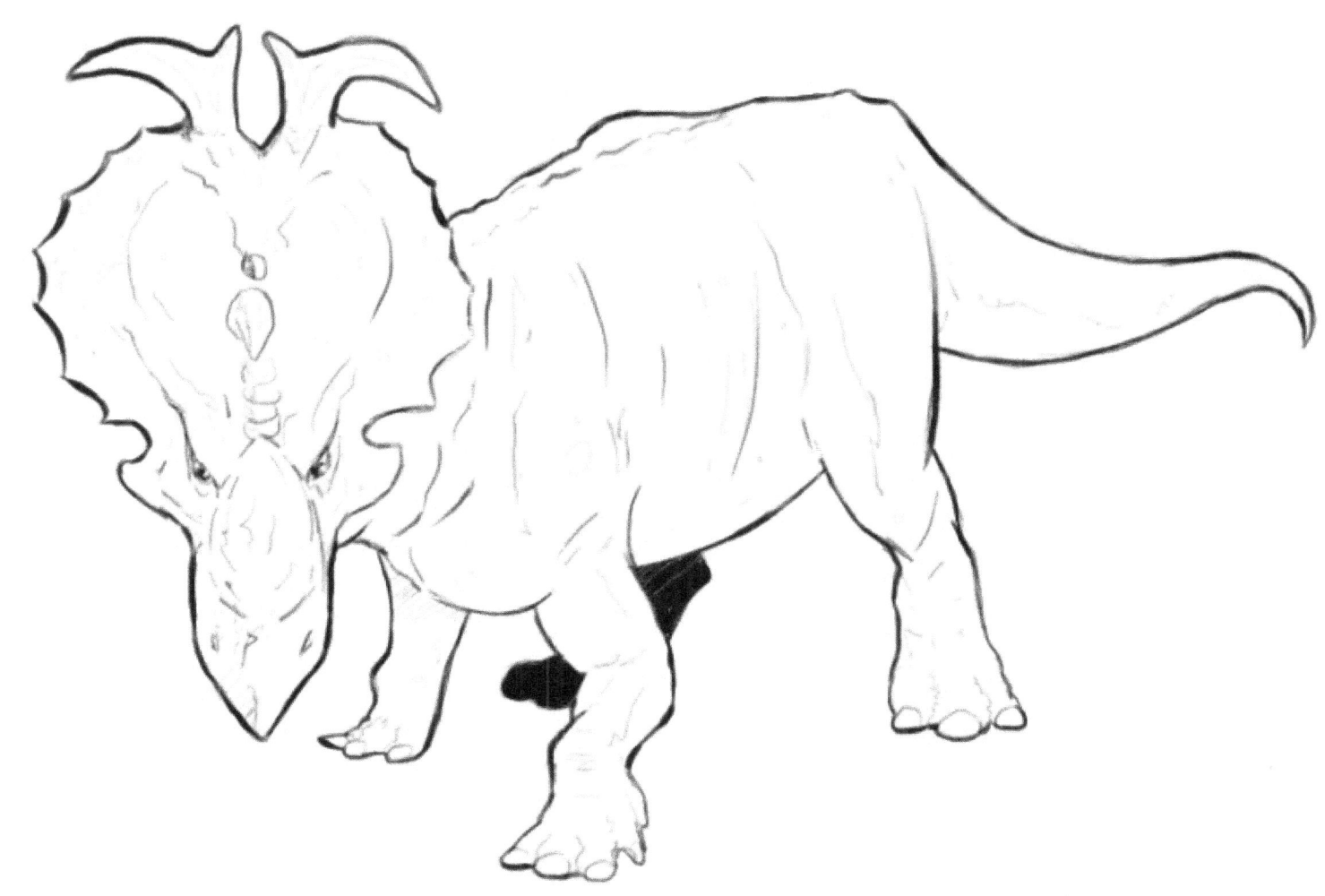

PACHYRHINOSAURUS

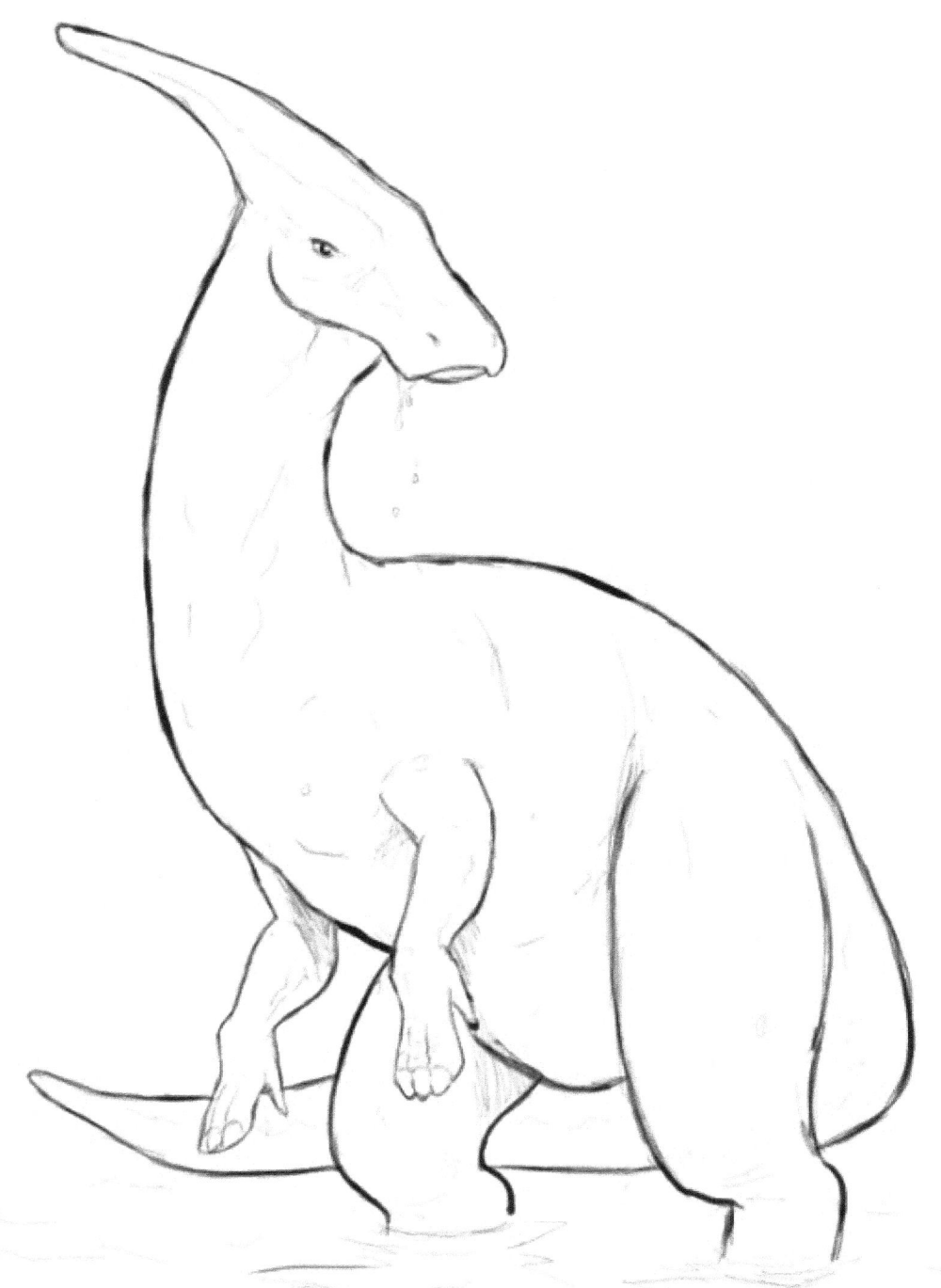

PARASAUROLOPHUS

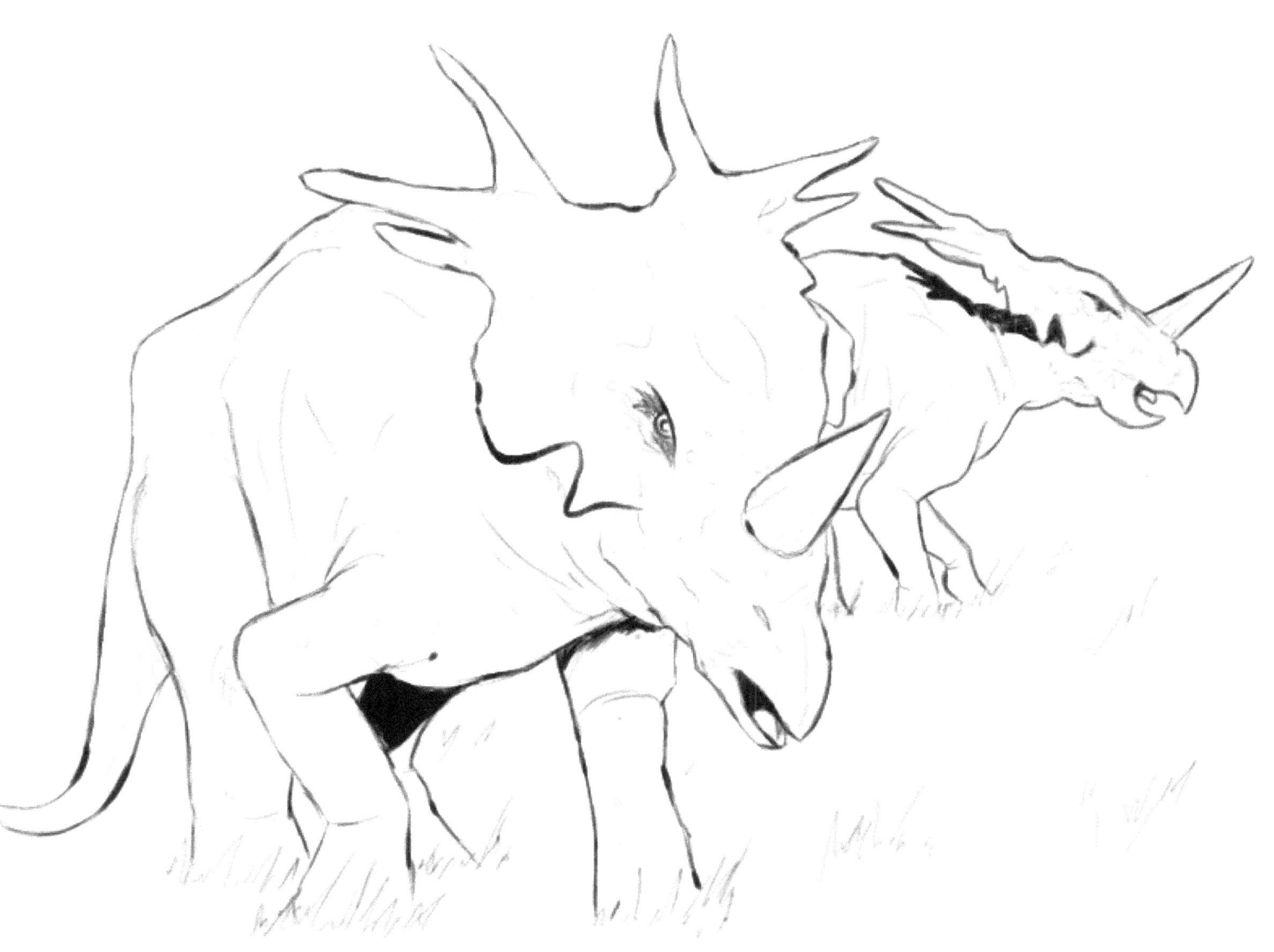

STYRACOSAURUS

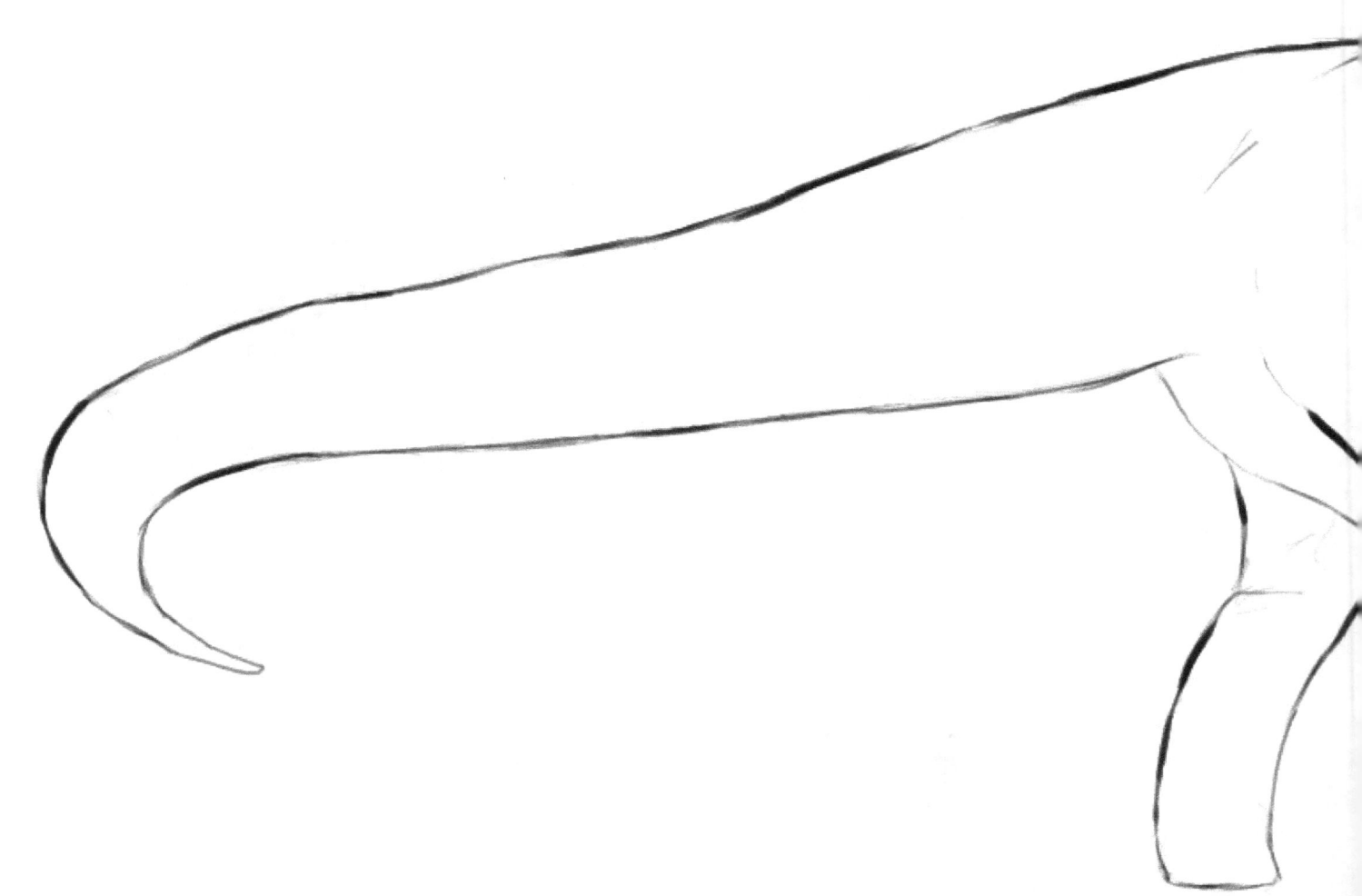

PATAGONIAN

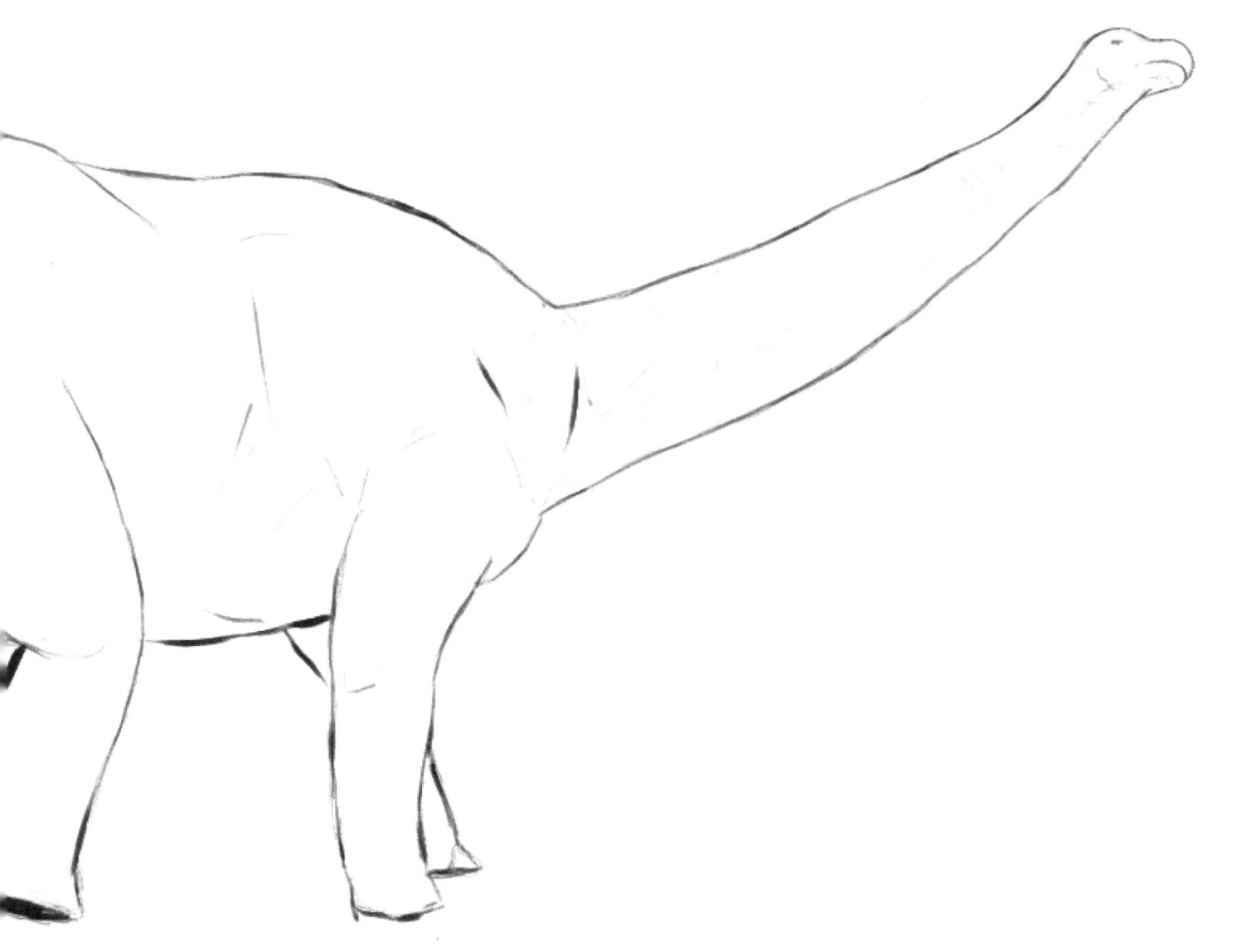

TITANOSAUR

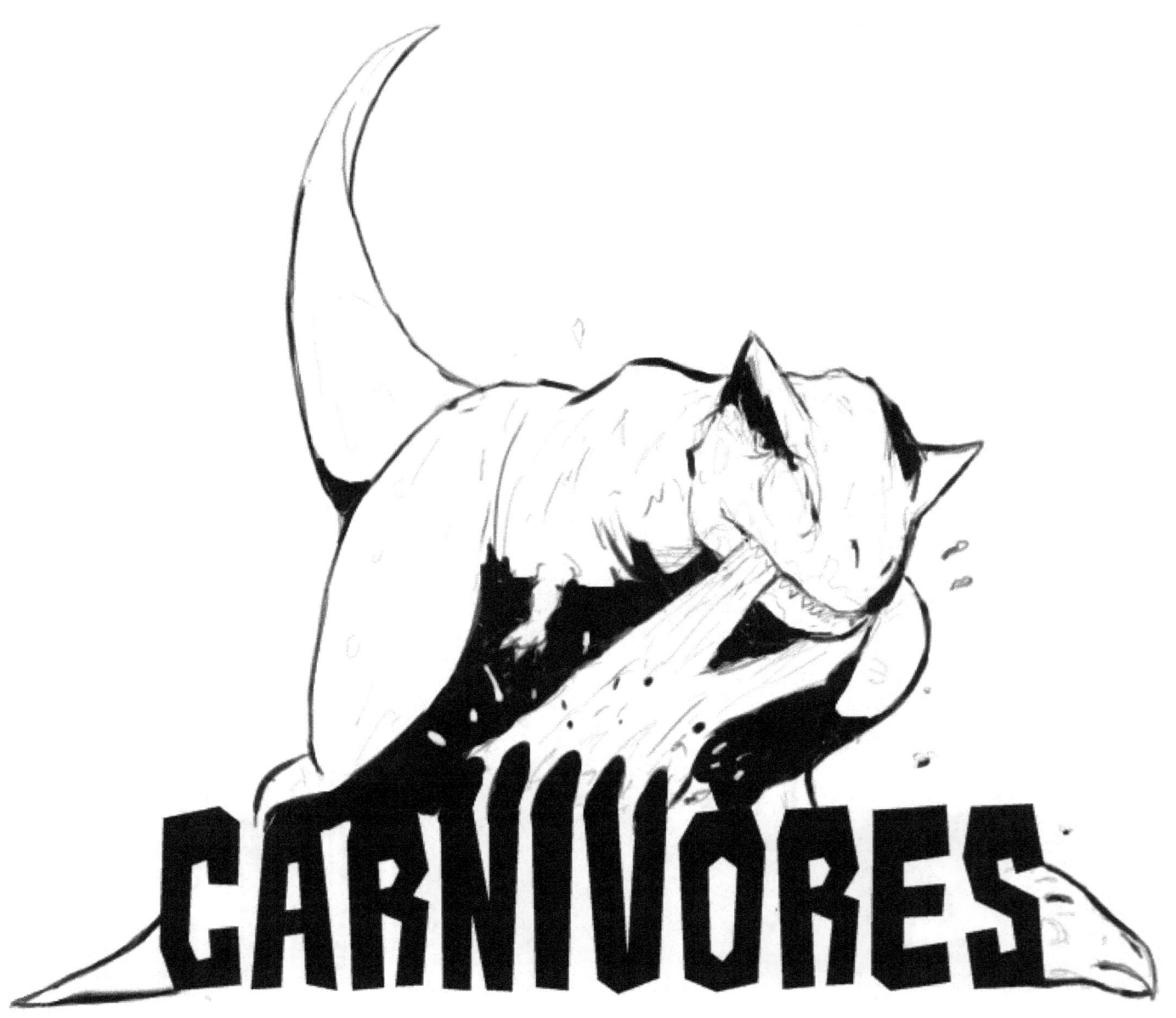

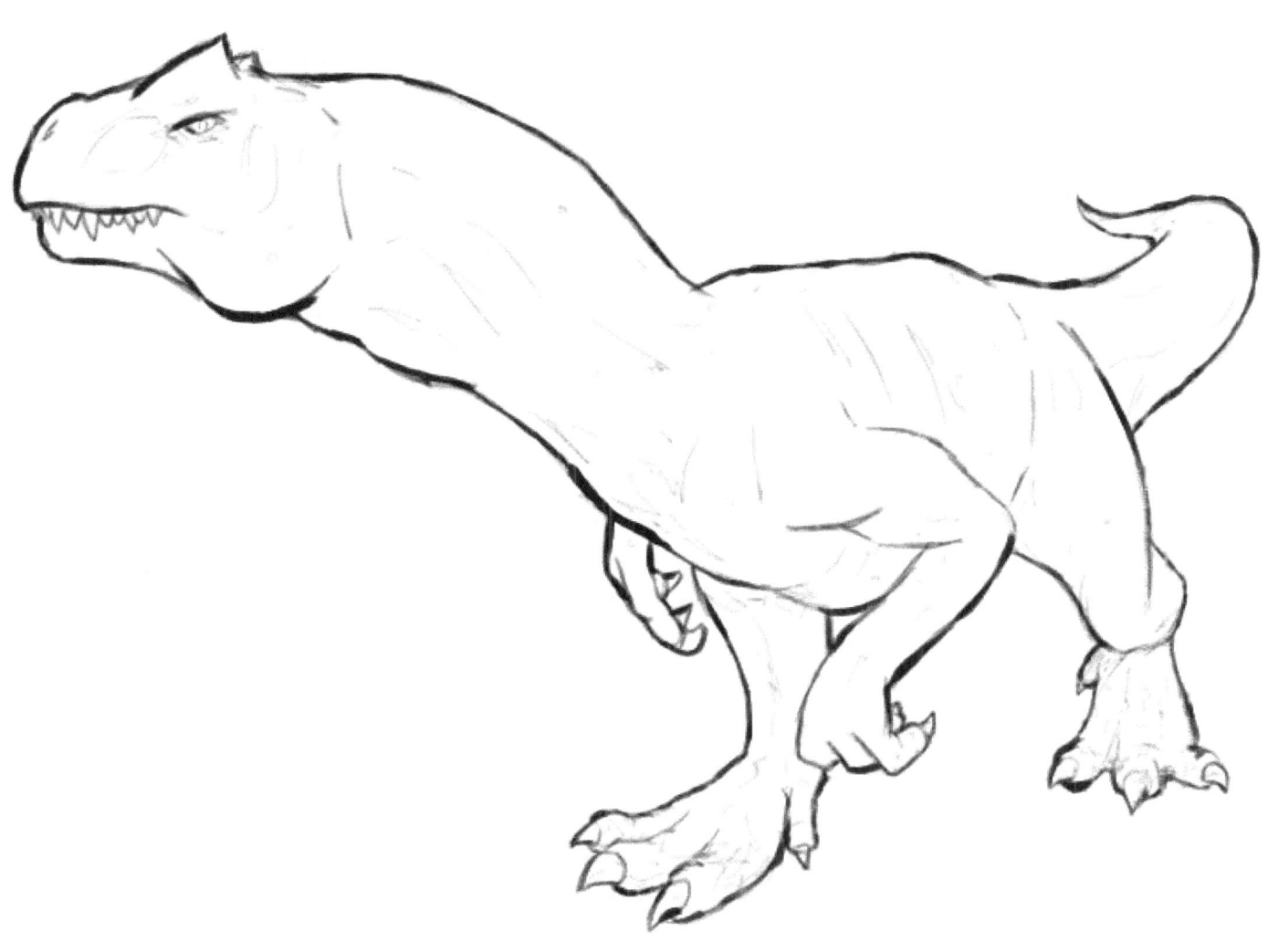

ALLOSAURUS

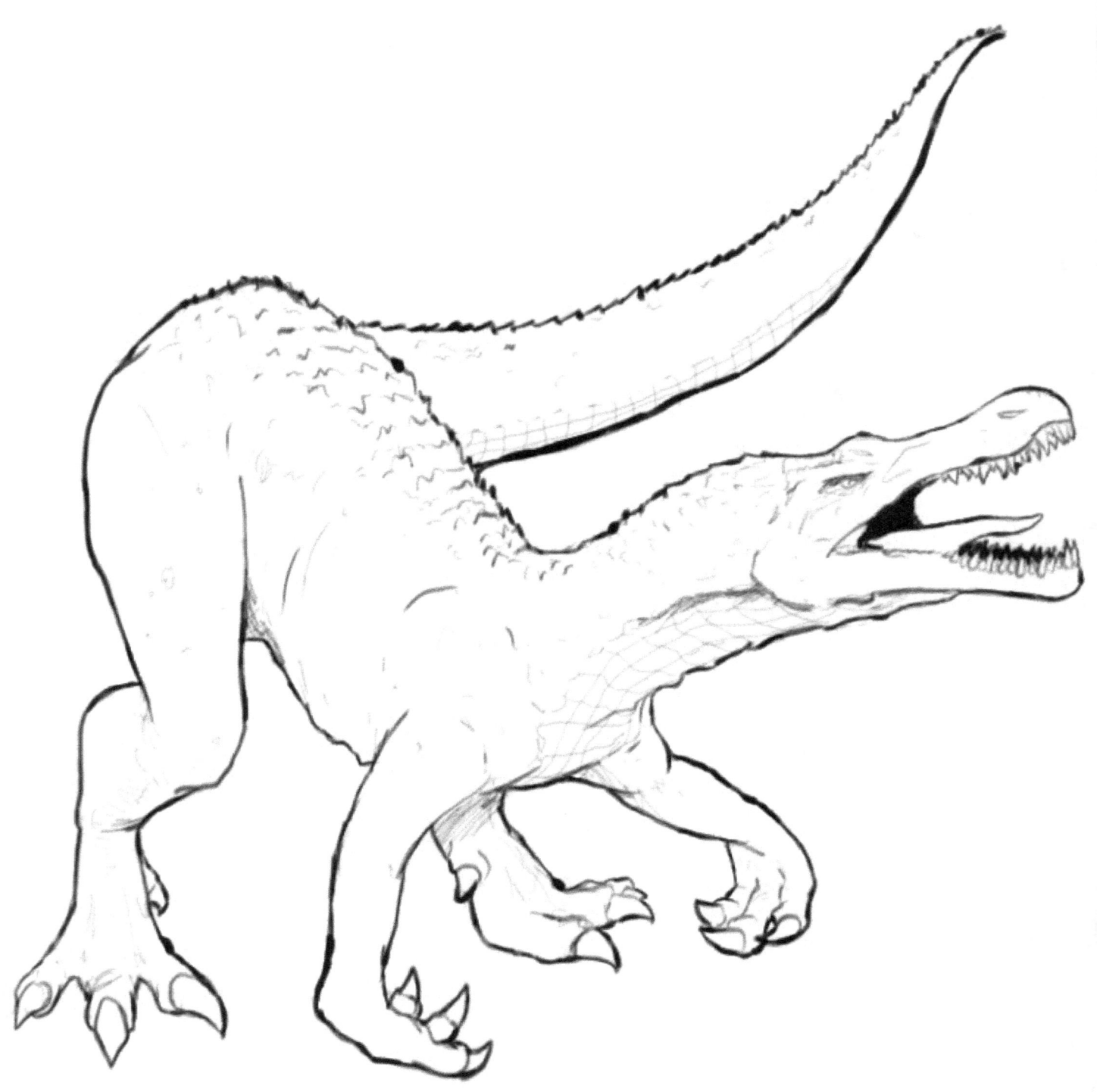

BARYONYX

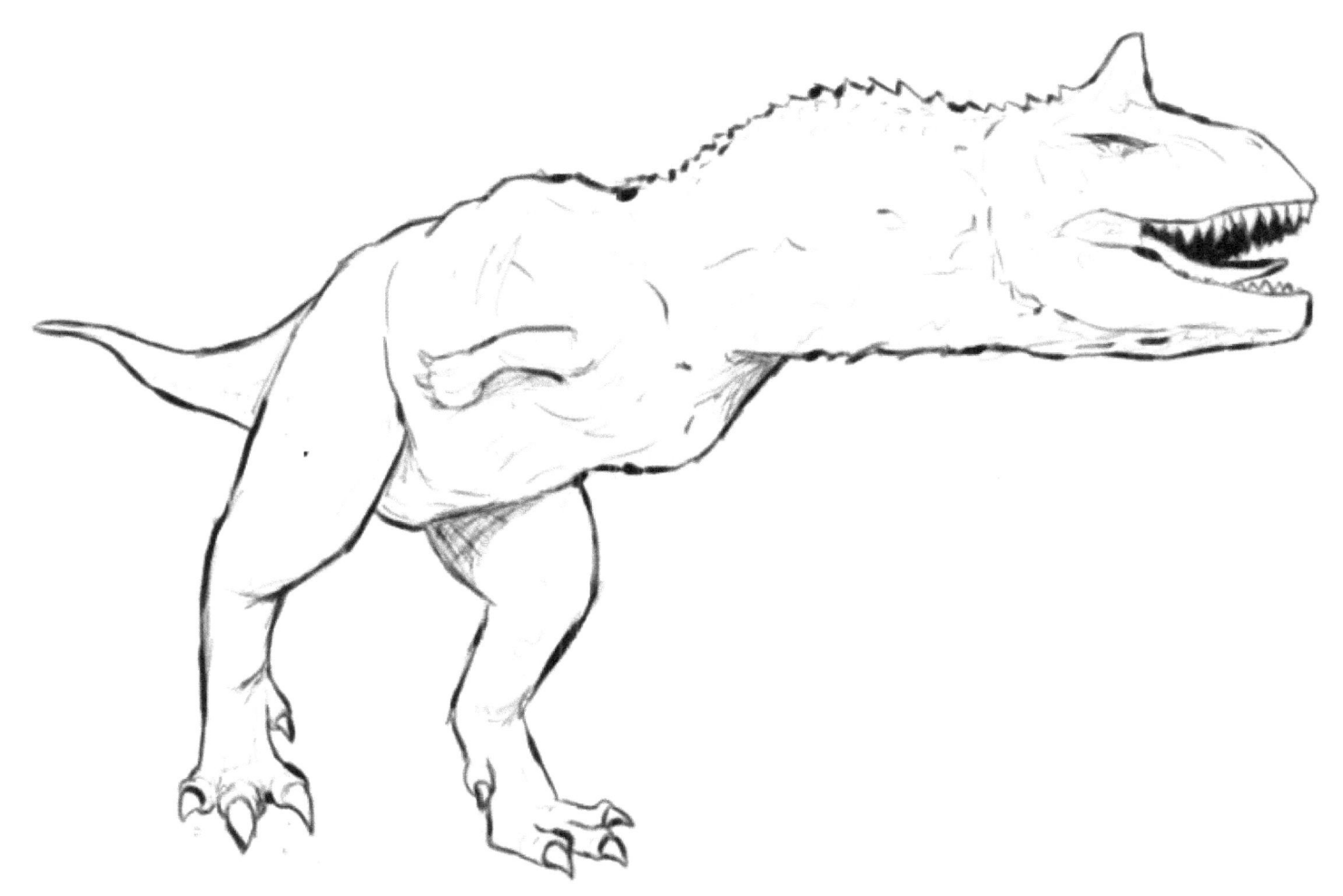

CARNOTAURUS

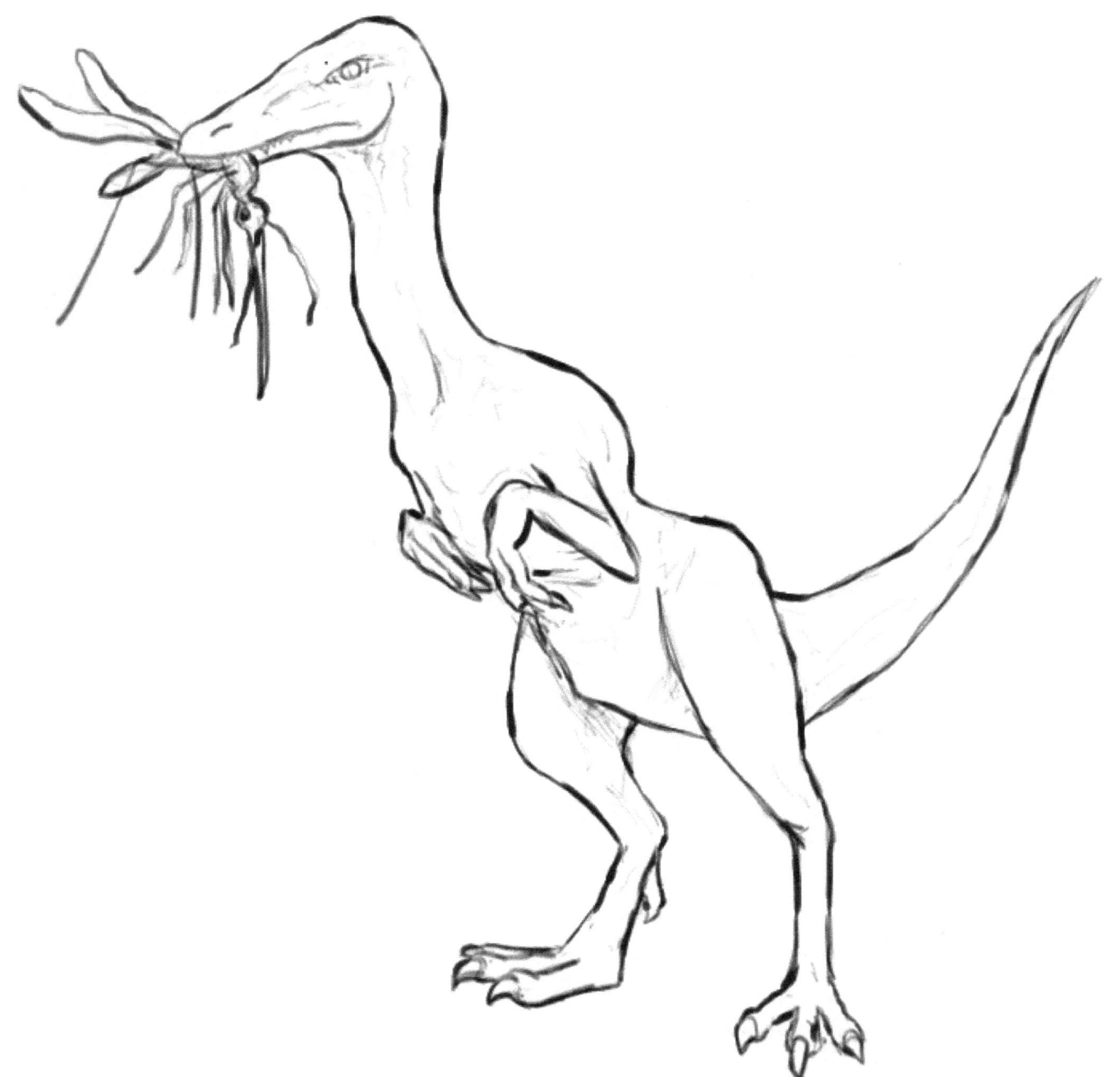

COMPSOGNATHUS

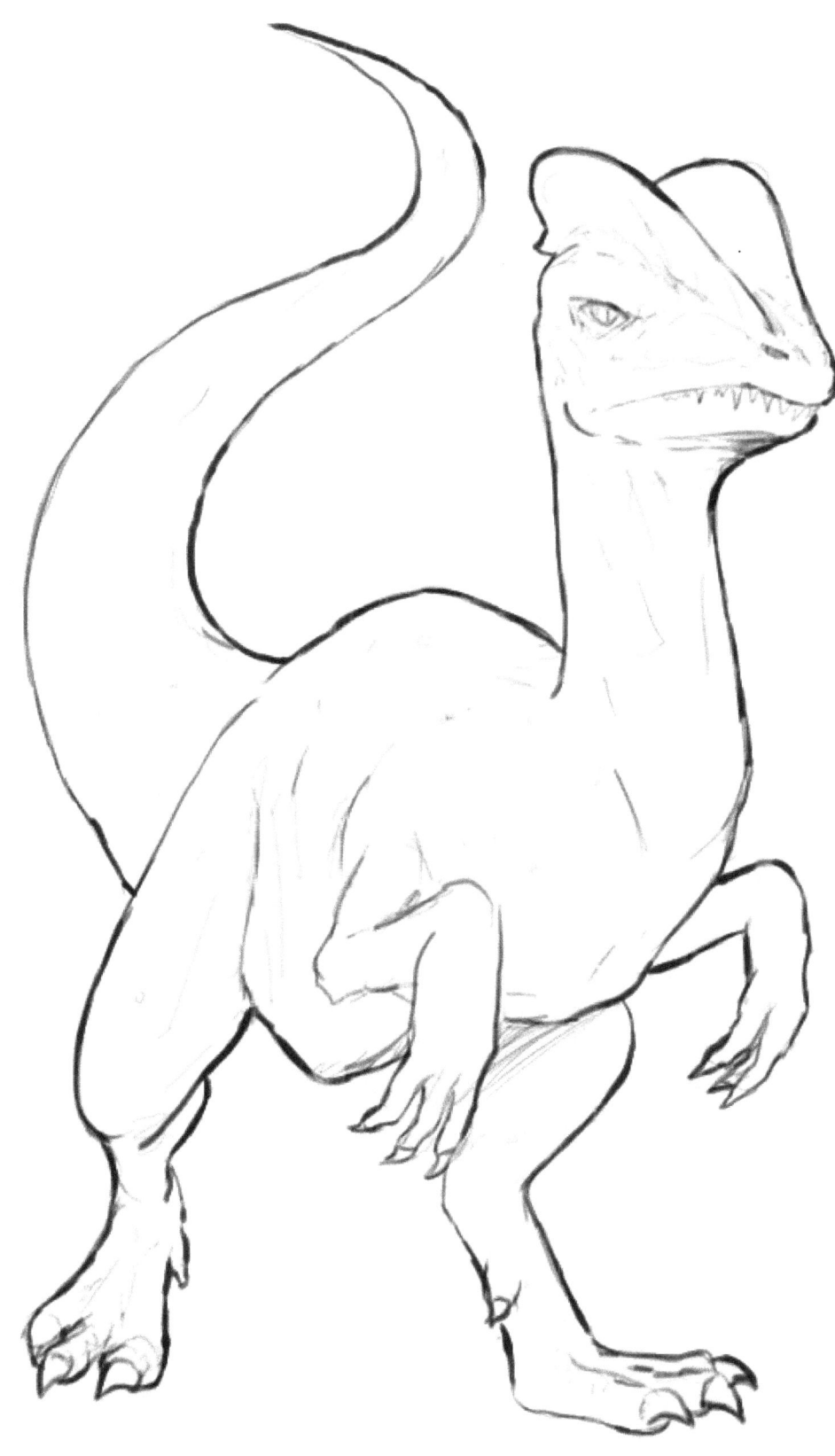

DILOPHOSAURUS

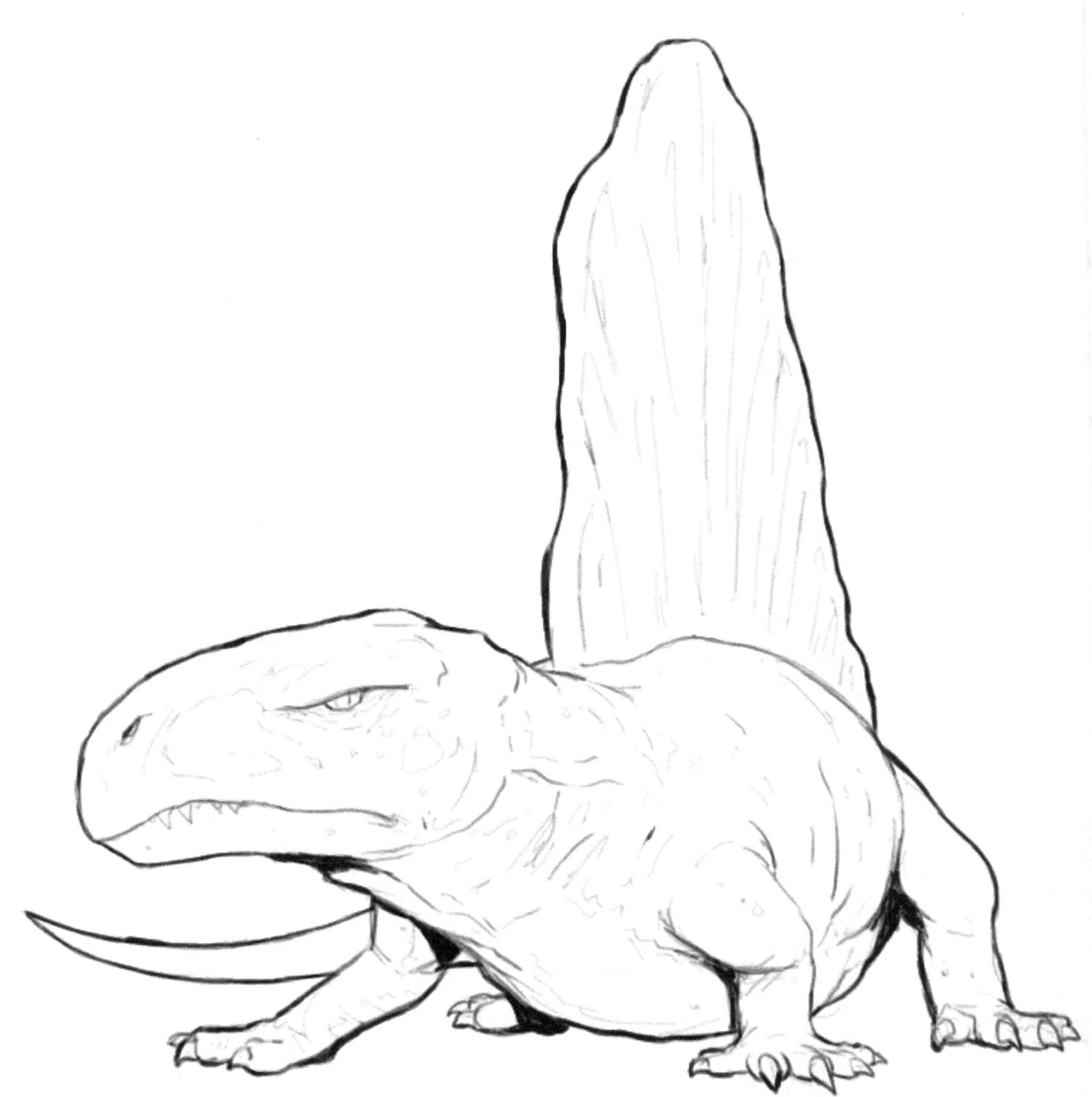

DIMETRODON

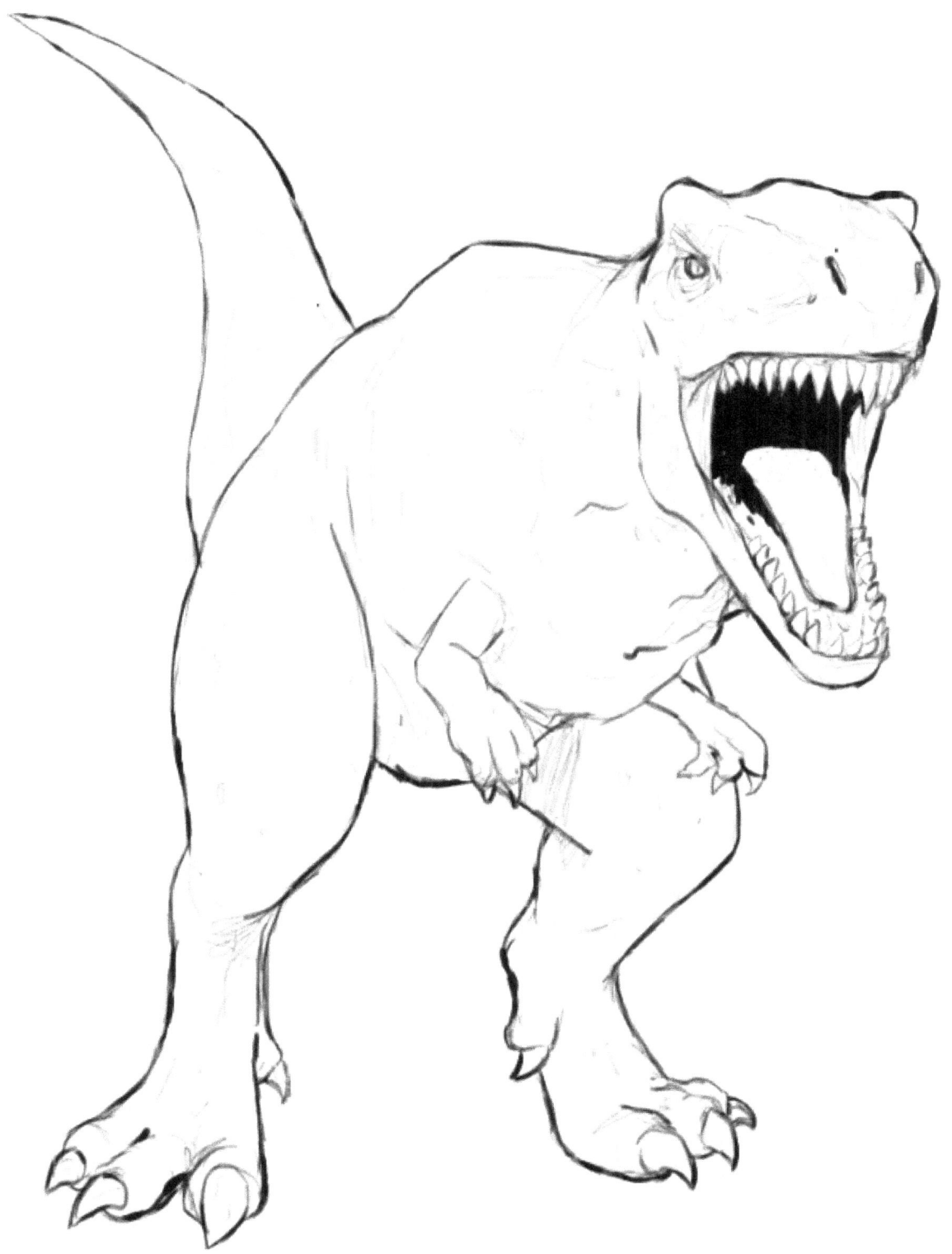

GIGANITOSAURUS

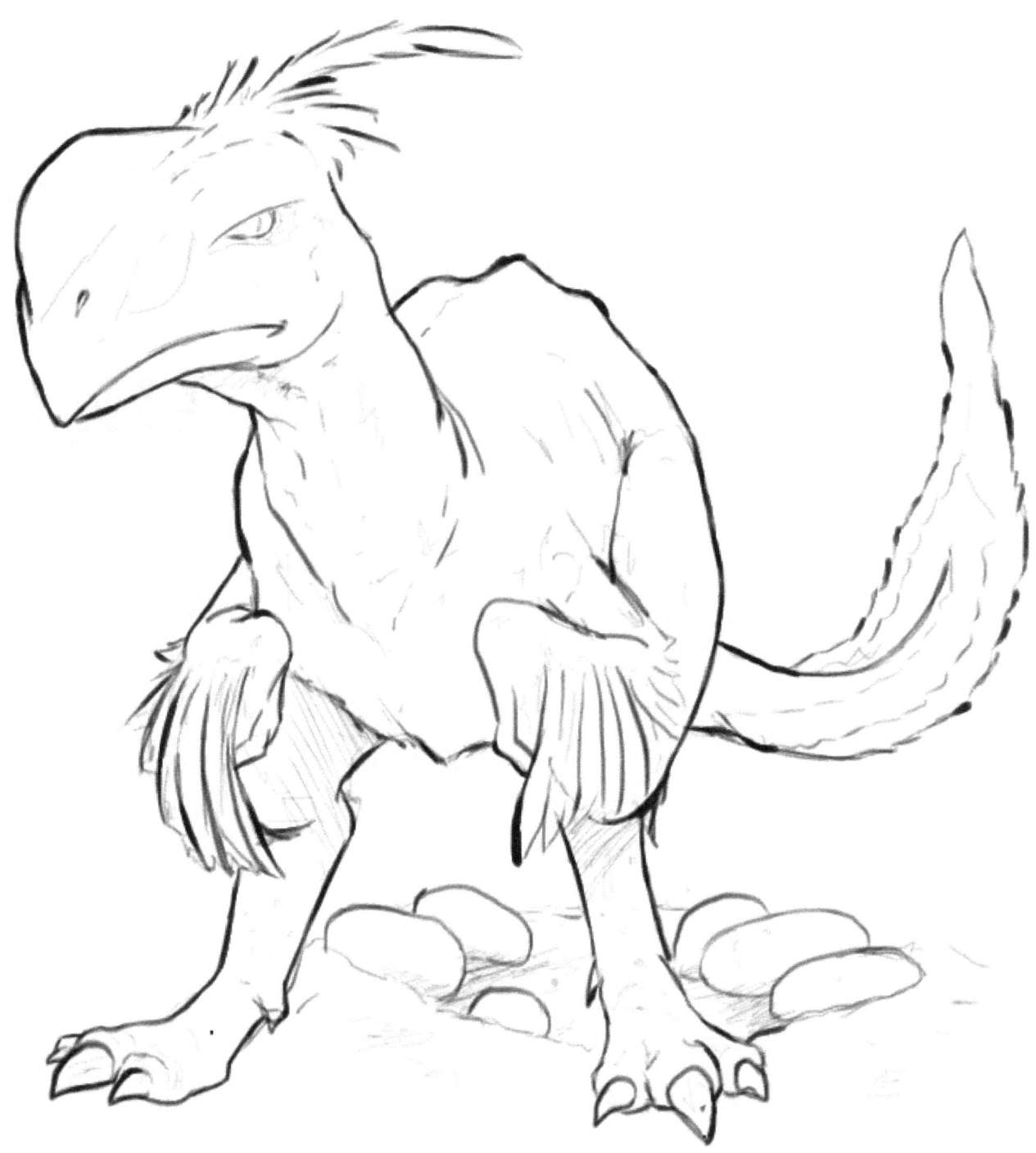

OVIRAPTOR

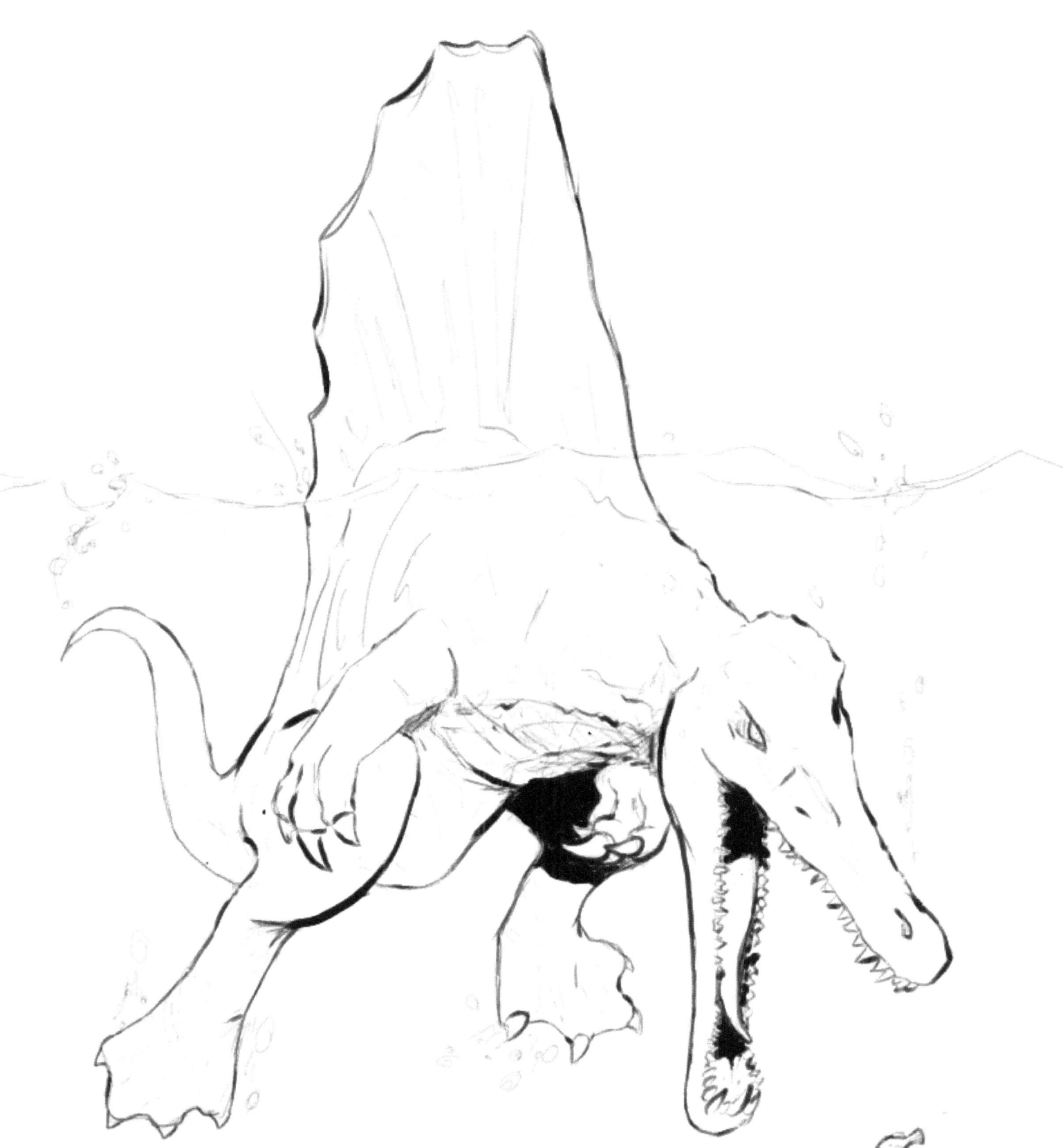

SPINOSAURUS

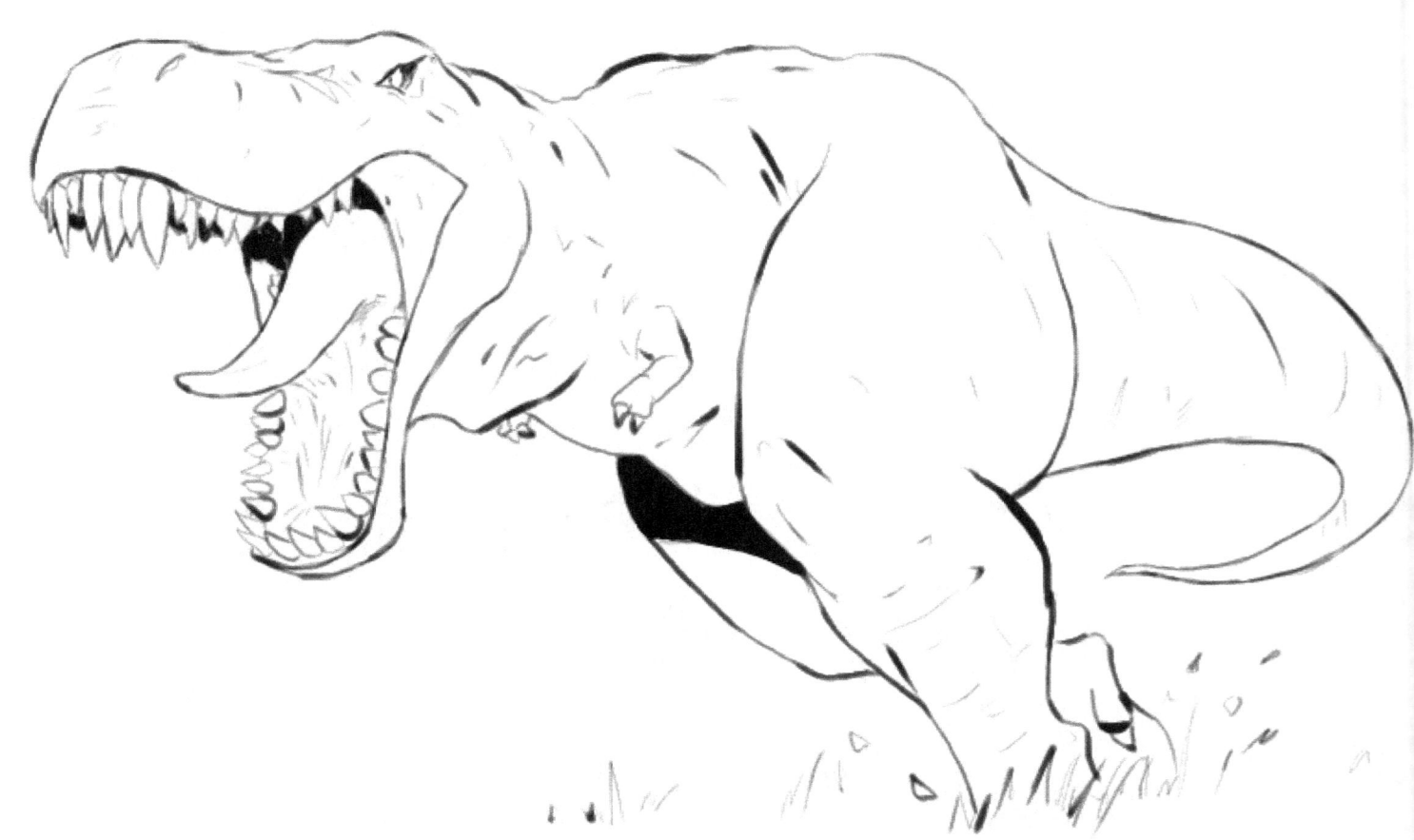

TYRANNOSAURUS REX

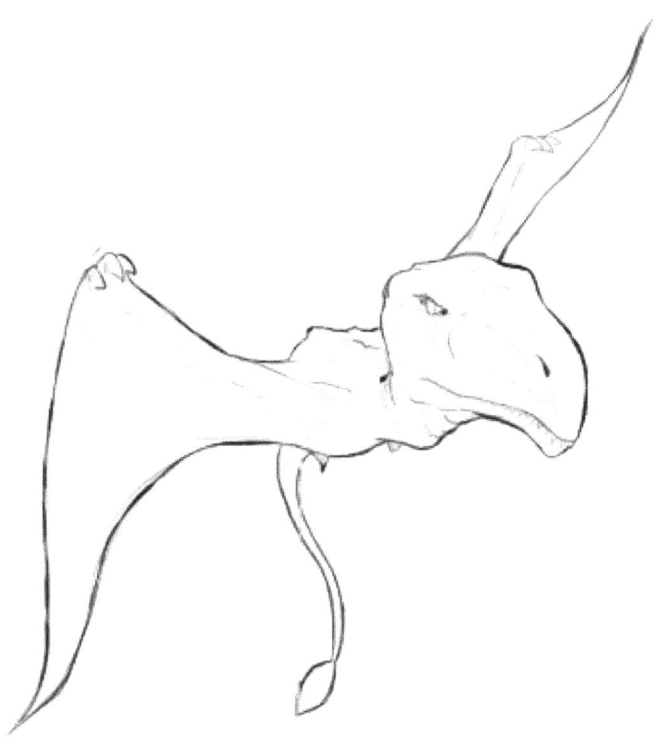

OTHER PREHISTORIC BEASTS

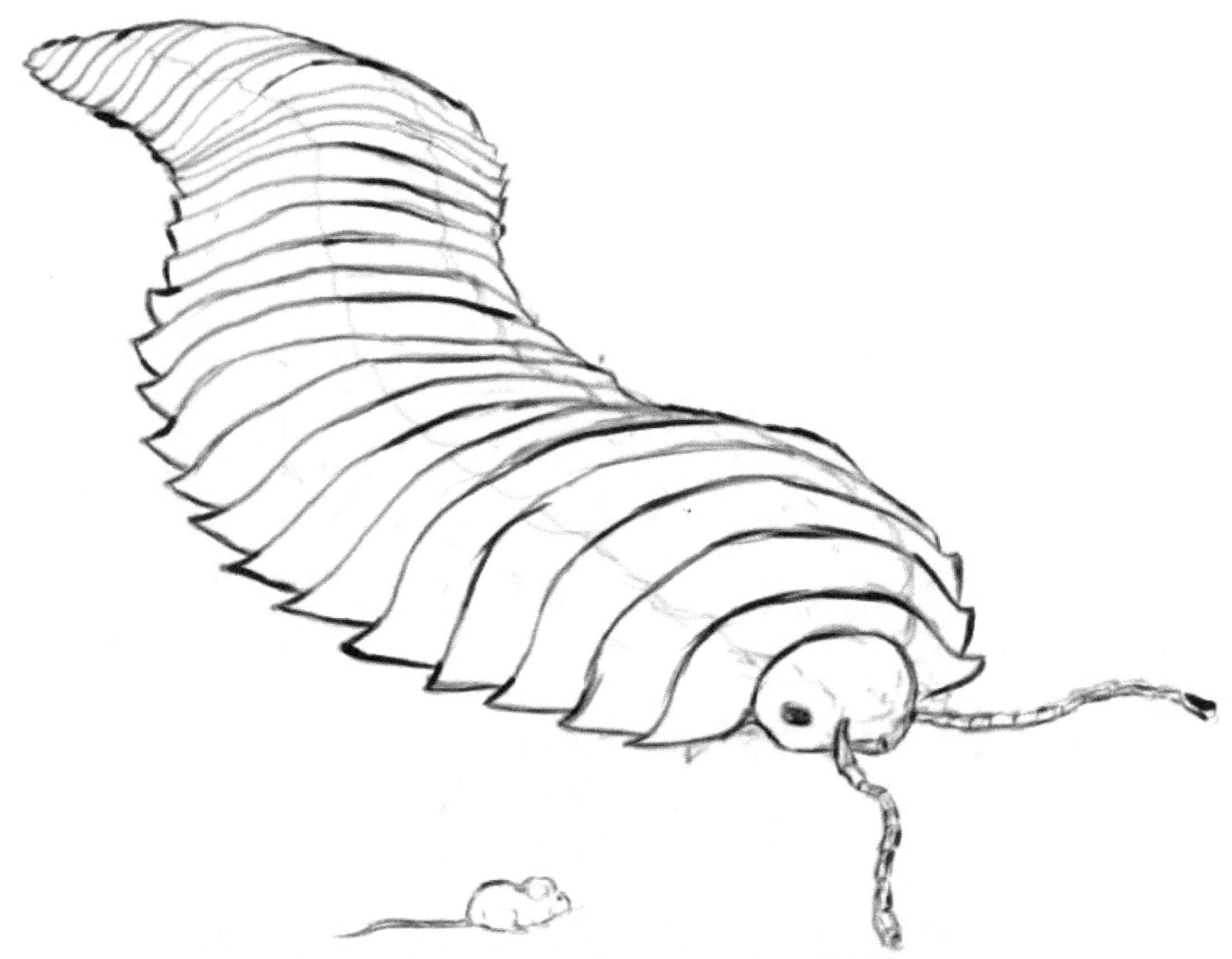

ANTHROPLEURA

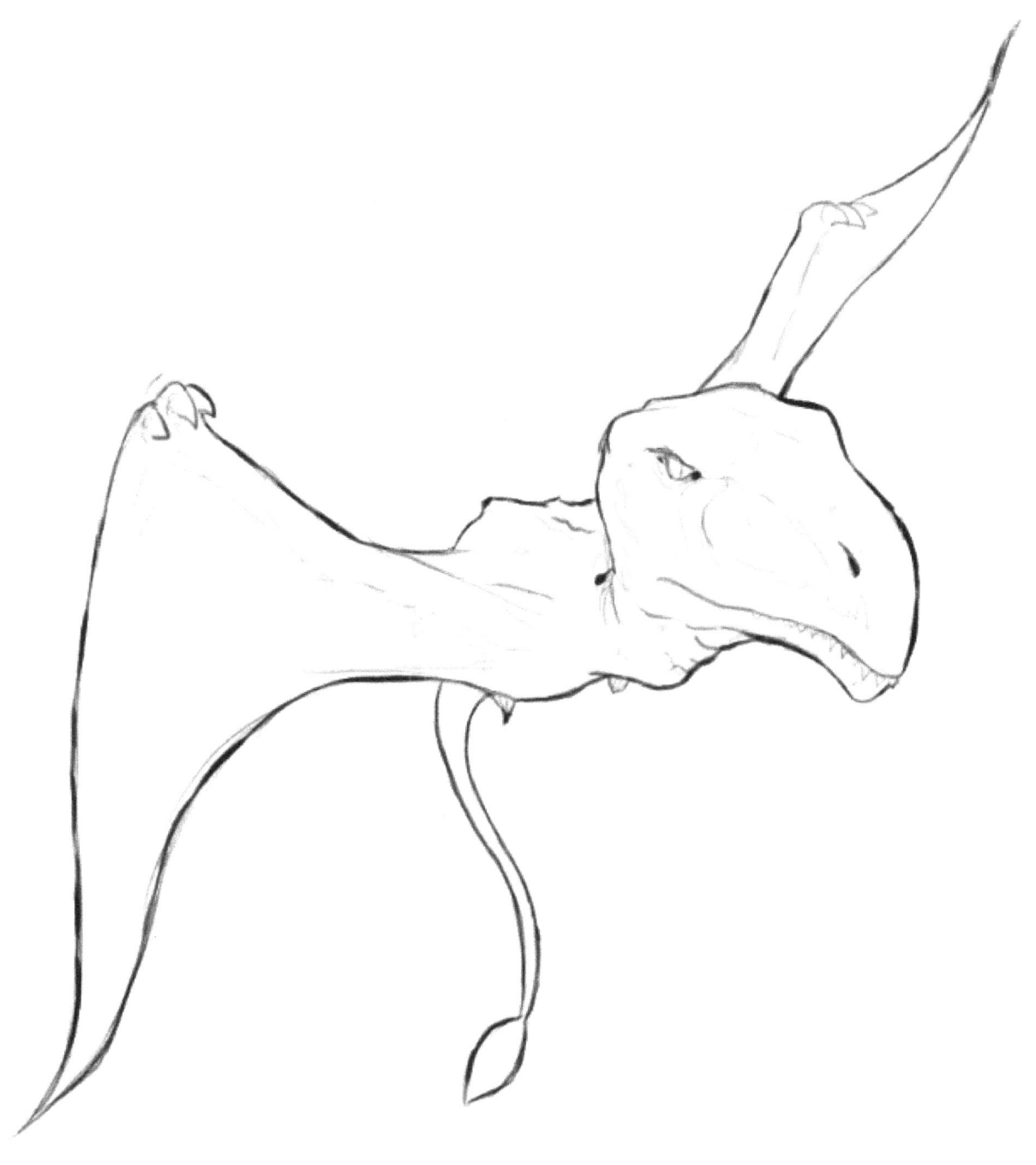

DIMORPHODON

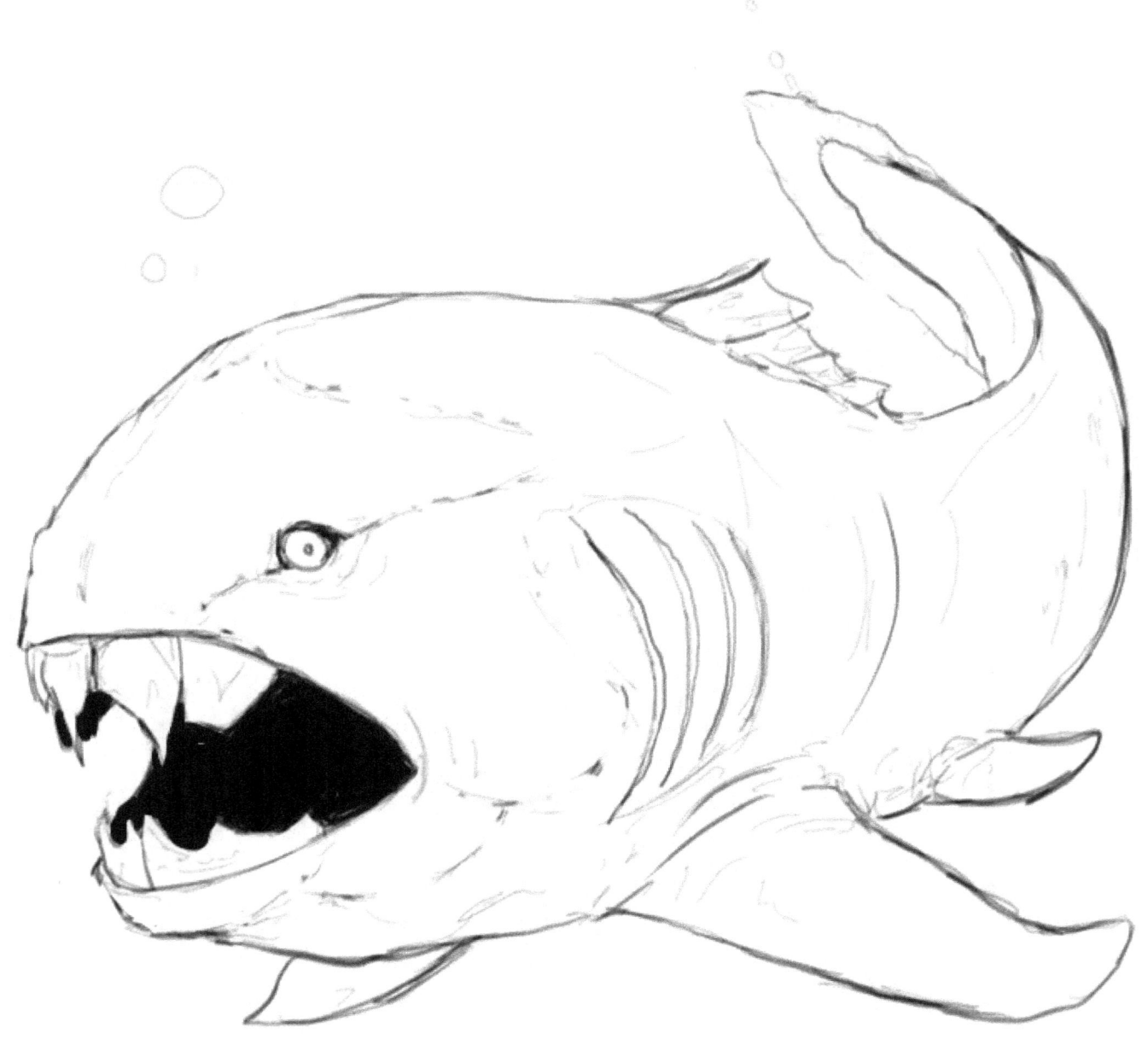

DUNKLEOSTEUS

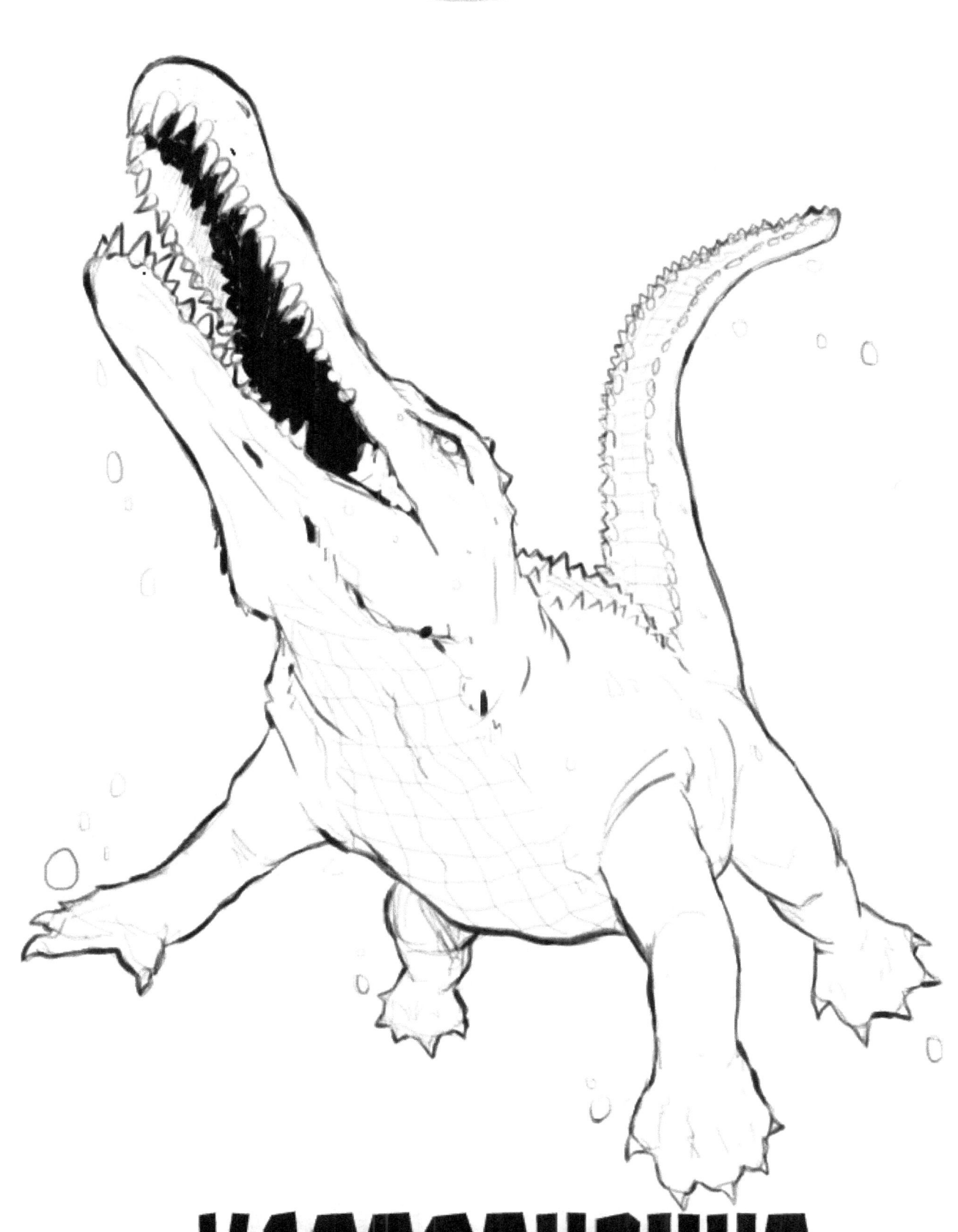

KAPROSUCHUS

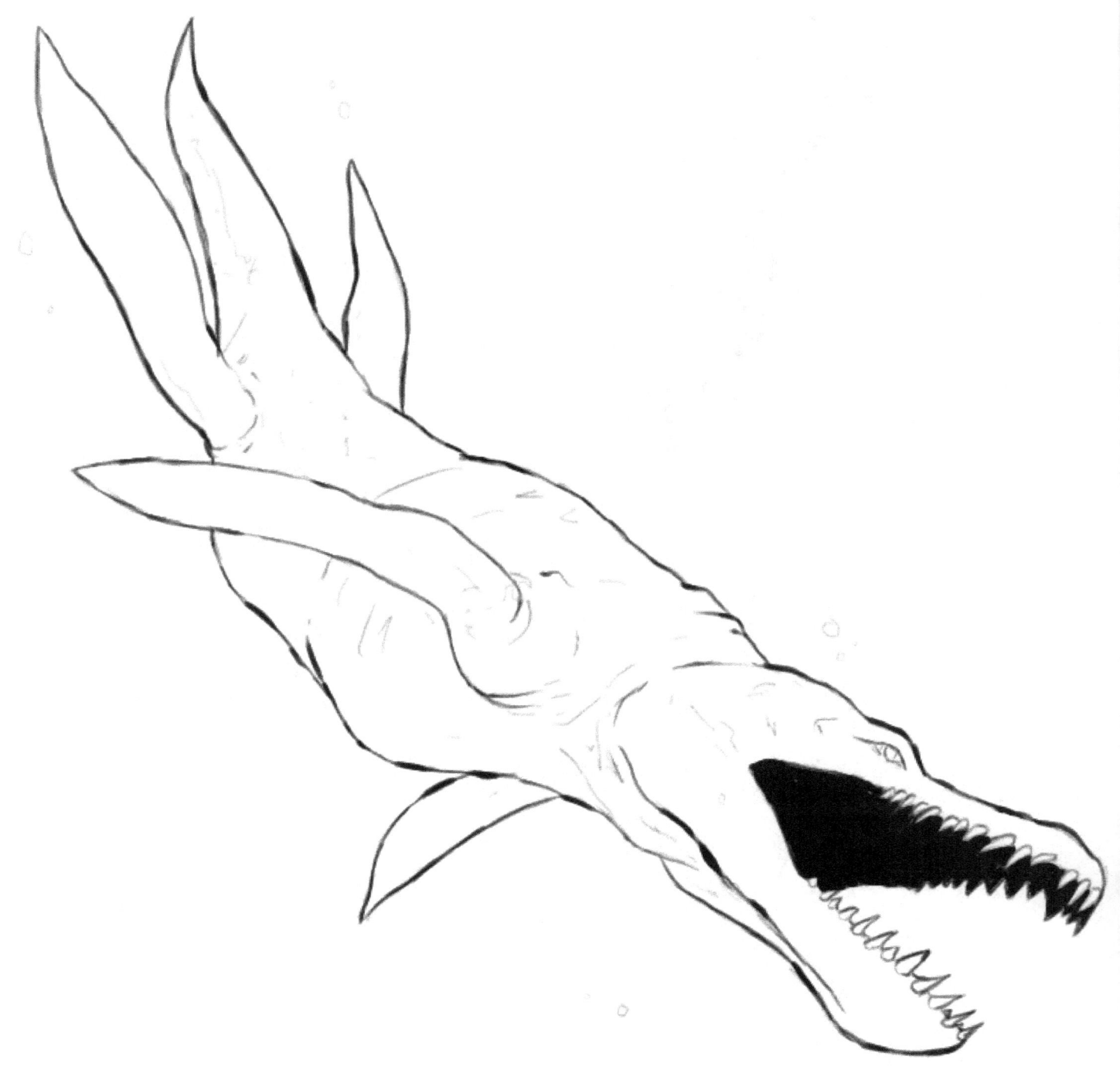

LIOPLEURODON

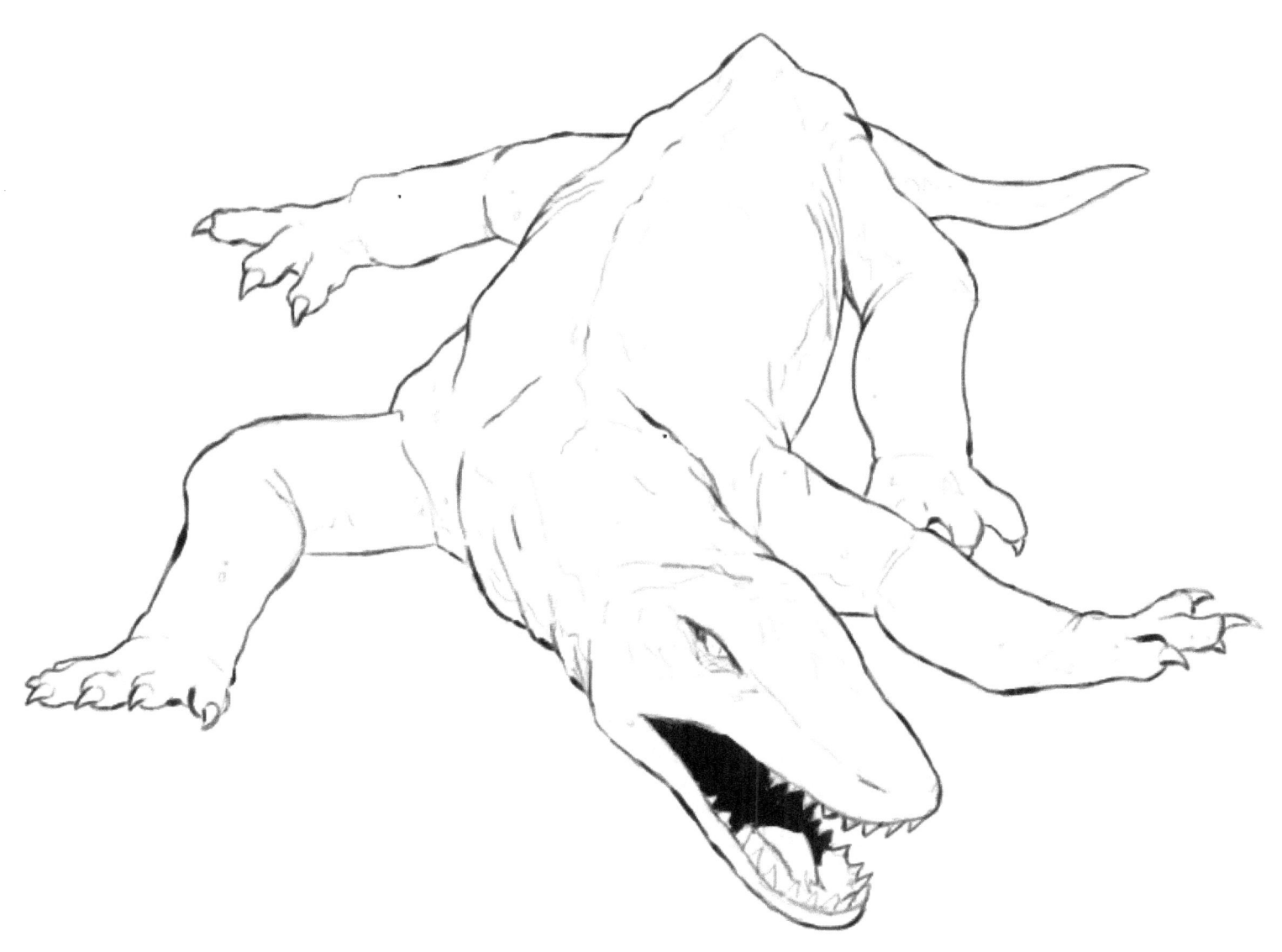

MEGALANIA

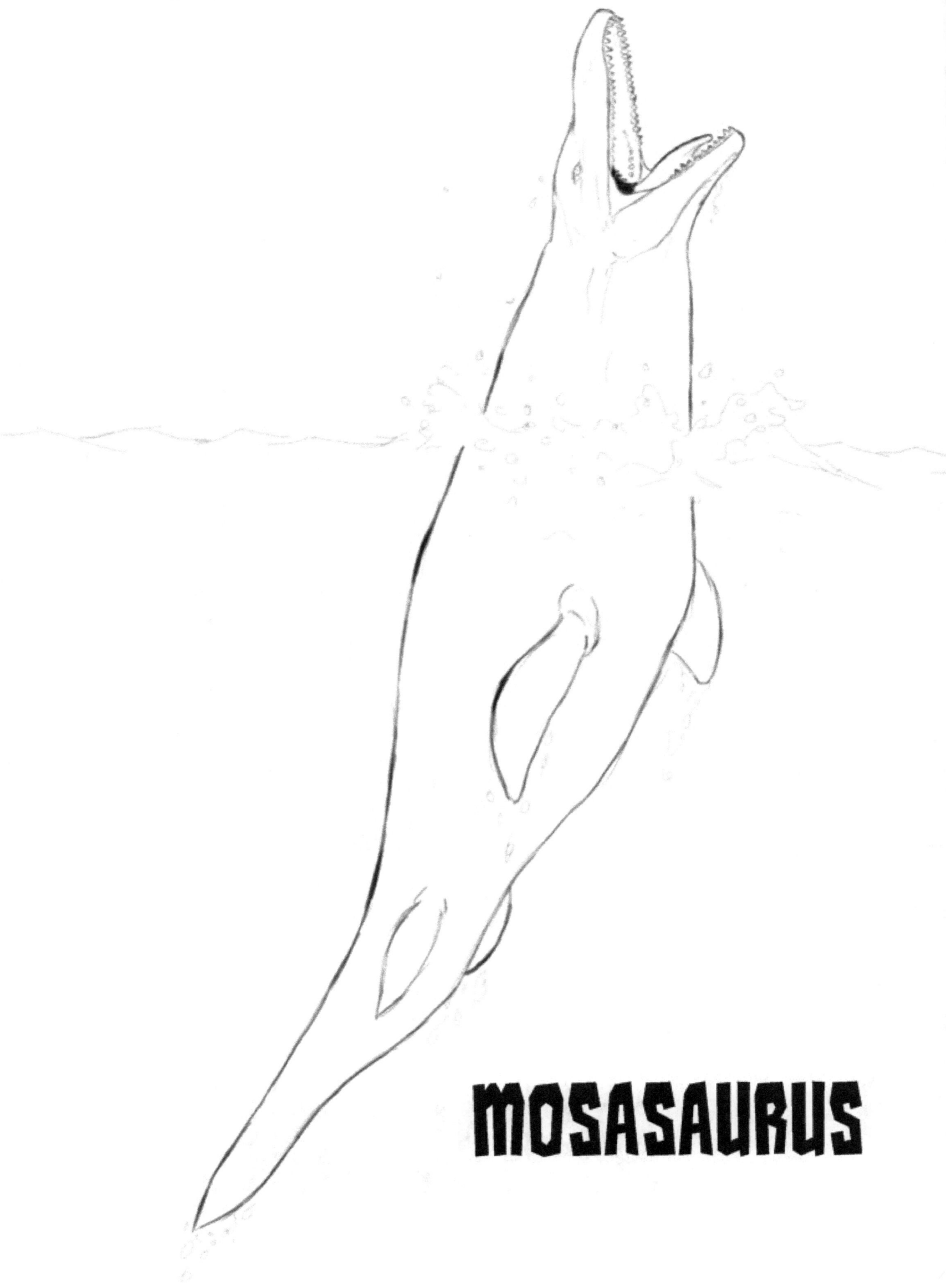

MOSASAURUS

PTERANODON

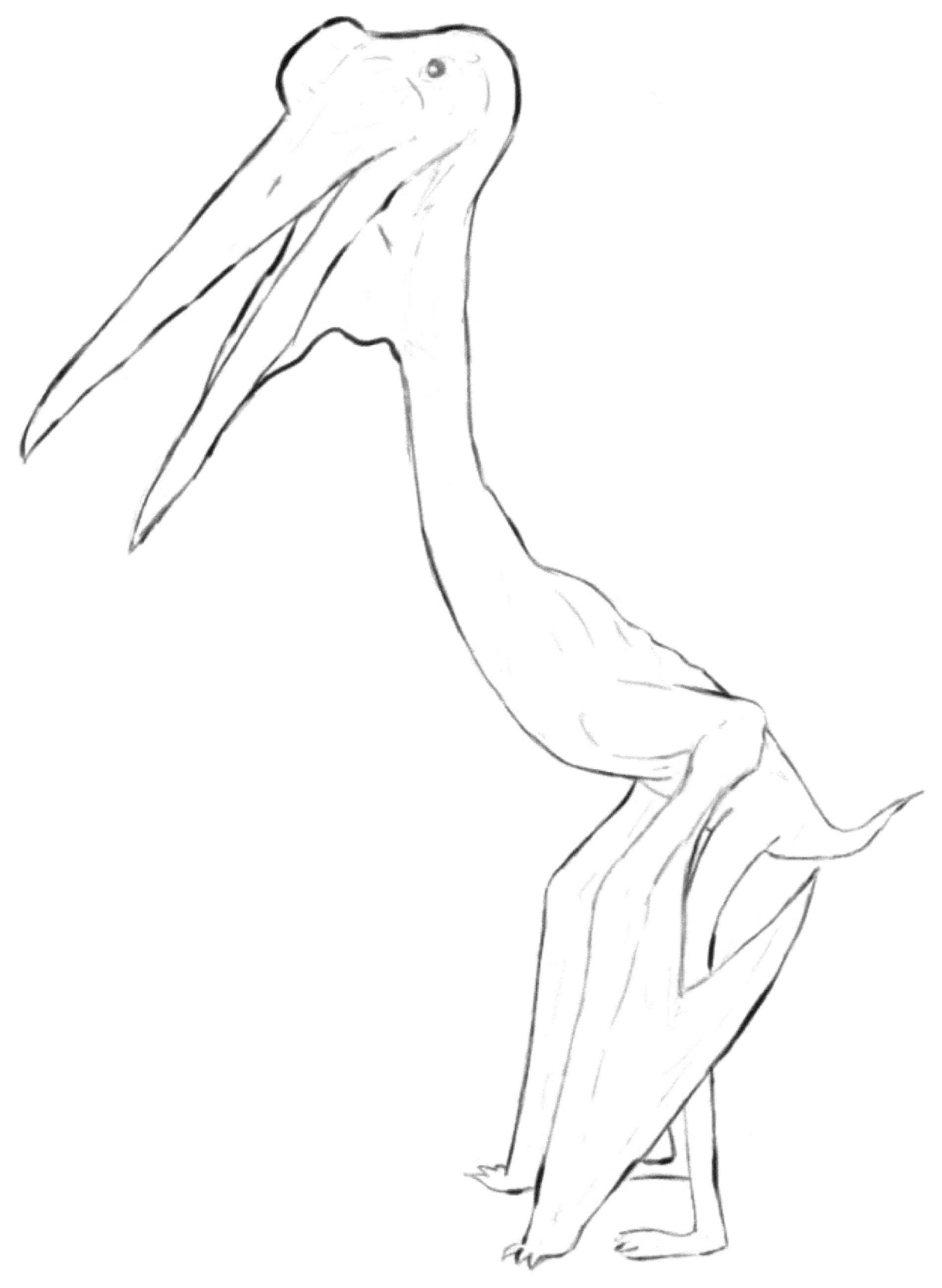

QEUTZALCOATLUS

www.ingramcontent.com/pod-product-compliance
Lightning Source LLC
Chambersburg PA
CBHW080537190526
45169CB00007B/2526